TO THE FOOT OF
THE RAINBOW

THE NATURAL WINDOW, CAÑON DE CHELLY

TO THE FOOT OF
THE RAINBOW

A TALE OF TWENTY-FIVE HUNDRED MILES
OF WANDERING ON HORSEBACK THROUGH
THE SOUTHWEST ENCHANTED LAND

BY CLYDE KLUCKHOHN

UNIVERSITY OF NEW MEXICO PRESS

ALBUQUERQUE

Library of Congress Cataloging-in-Publication Data

Kluckhohn, Clyde, 1905-1960
To the foot of the rainbow : a tale of twenty-five hundred miles
of wandering on horseback through
the southwest enchanted land / by Clyde Kluckhohn.
p.   cm.
Originally published : New York : Century Co., c1927.
ISBN 0-8263-1342-6
1. Indians of North America—Southwest,
New—Social life and customs.
2. Southwest, New—Description and travel.
I. Title.
E78.S7K57   1992
979'.00497—dc20   91-40559

This volume contains the complete text
and illustrations of the first edition, published in 1927.

University of New Mexico Press edition, 1992.

TO

LOWELL AND JACK

PARTNERS IN NAVAJO-LAND

. . . AND ELSEWHERE

ACKNOWLEDGMENT

Dr. Matthews's translation of the Indian song in the last chapter is taken by permission from a report of the Bureau of American Ethnology. Two other translations, which are indicated by foot-notes, are from "The Indians' Book," by Natalie Curtis (copyright 1907 by Natalie Curtis, copyright 1923 by Paul Burlin, published by Harper & Brothers).

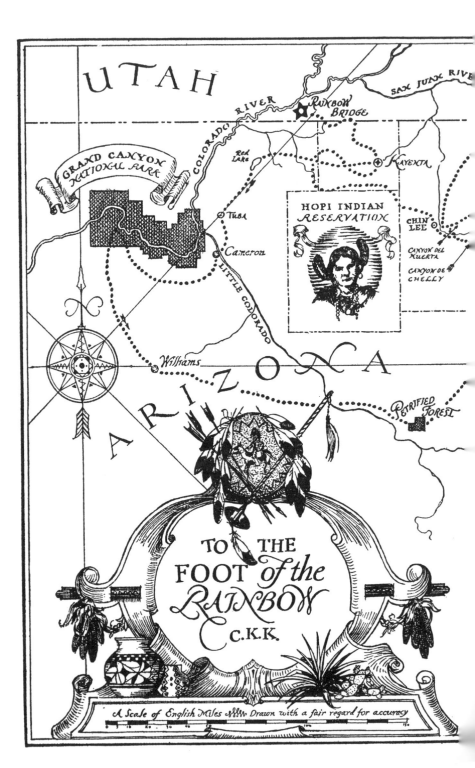

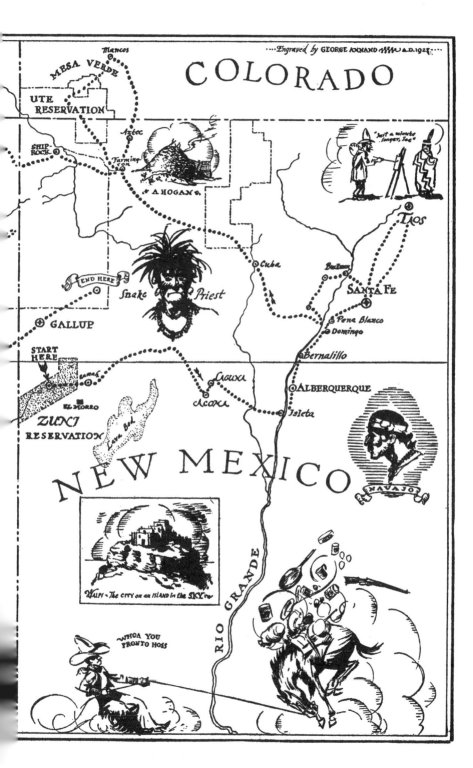

CONTENTS

TO THE FOOT OF
THE RAINBOW

L. E. HATLEY & SON

DEALERS IN

LIVE STOCK
HEREFORD CATTLE

CATTLE LEFT SIDE
HORSES LEFT THIGH

RAMAH, N. M.,

June 7th, 1923.

This is to certify that I have this day sold to
Clyde K. Kluckhohn one three year hold bay horse
with white star on face branded ⟨✦ for a
consideration of $35.00.

L. E. Hatley.
By Sam. Hatley.

Clyde Kluckhohn

Albert Vogt

Tom Scruggs

TO THE FOOT
OF THE RAINBOW

I

H OW we had cursed the scrubby cedars and piñons which had obscured our view as we were ascending, but now from the whole we recoiled in fear. We were truly afraid. The abject impulse of physical terror which we had felt on first looking down that cruel jagged precipice was succeeded by mental terror far more profound and soul-pervading. The finiteness of our minds balked at the immensity of the scene; our emotions were akin to those of Psyche when she looked upon Divinity and was blinded. Here was the whole landscape whose phases we had intimately known, and yet how different—all blended and mingled so that we were unable even to identify those specific glories of nature with which we were most fa-

miliar. Here as an entity was the vision which
had been tantalizingly disclosed to us in brief
vistas as we were toilsomely worming our way up
the trail which corkscrews dizzily up the precipitous wall of To-yo-a-lan-a, the sacred Thunder
Mountain of the Zuñi Indians.

We could not move; we looked and looked,
and finally out of the greens and blues and grays
we could distinguish. At the very end of the
western horizon is a definitive blue spectrum—
the White Mountains of Arizona, more than one
hundred miles distant—while to the rear and
much closer is the ragged metallic blue outline of
the Zuñi Mountains rising against the turquoise
New Mexican sky. Immediately below, To-yo-a-
lan-a casts its shadow upon the irrigated green
valley surrounding adobe-terraced Zuñi pueblo,
while to the other side of the valley, and separated from it by the thread-like Zuñi River,
writhes the desert where the restless spirits must
wander forever; above its waves of sand, towers
Has Ta No Gi, the spectral rock, which looks
like a phantom ship that is chained motionless by
its own desire to sail so many ways.

There on the very edge of Thunder Mountain,

a thousand feet above the plain, Evon Vogt and Zuñi Nick and I made our camp amid the dry, clean, sweet fragrance of the cedar timber. And when the evening cool began to nip our ears, and we could hear the howl of the coyote so near, Evon began the customary camp-fire story:

"Did I ever tell you about the Penitente Brothers? No? Well, it was just twenty years ago this month that I first came into contact with them—not more than a year after they sent me away from the university to the Southwest because I was threatened with T.B.—I believe I told you that. After a few weeks in a sanatorium, I started to knock about, and soon became a sheep-herder along with the Mexicans. With them I became pretty intimate, and before long I heard from some of them of this Penitente order, which, it seems, was once very numerous in New Mexico but had been gradually stamped out by the church and government, until only a very few active bands in out-of-the-way hamlets were left; now there are but two, I think. I suppose this brotherhood is a direct but perverted descendant of the penitent orders of the Middle Ages; its membership here is made up of the most ignorant Mexicans, for, despite the teachings of the Church, they believe that by being an active Penitente they will obtain everlasting remission of their sins. For this reason the organization has always been popular with murderers and those guilty of mortal sin.

"But I am digressing from my story. I heard that the Penitente brotherhood was going to stage its Holy Week rites at San Mateo, not far from where we were then herding, and I asked Felipe Chávez if he couldn't take me over. At first he disclaimed all knowledge of the existence of the order, then he said he dared not take an American, but eventually he agreed to take me there late Thursday evening.

"We went directly to the house of the *hermano mayor,* or eldest brother, where the whole brotherhood was assembled. I can't ever forget the scene I beheld on first entering that room—a dozen Mexicans, stripped to the waist, kneeling and praying, while lay brothers flogged their backs with ropes, whips, aloe scourges, cactus swords. Soon there was an even more gruesome spectacle: two initiates came forward to receive the final symbol of the admission—they knelt before the *hermano mayor*—he raised aloft a stone knife and prayed aloud—then he swooped down with the knife and cut three gashes in the back of each candidate—salt was rubbed into the wounds, while they shrieked in pain.

"They went on with unspeakable rites—such as laying themselves on beds of cactus—for another hour or more until it was exactly midnight. Then all was suddenly silent. They gathered round the *hermano mayor*. He passed a hat containing paper pellets; they were drawing for the privilege of being crucified in the morning. The Penitentes hold that he who is crucified in commemoration of Christ will be sure of a place in heaven. But on this occasion the young fellow who received the slip with 'Christe' written upon it collapsed utterly and fainted.

"In the dim gray of early Good Friday morning the procession formed in the street in front of the house of the *hermano mayor*. The Christus, crowned with a cactus wreath, had a piñon cross strapped to his back; surrounding him were the other Penitentes. They moved forward, while the lay brothers flogged the active members and strewed cacti and thistles for them to tread upon with naked feet. And now the women were present too, and their screaming and moaning and shouting made the scene indescribable. At last they dragged themselves to the top of a hill outside the village; there the cross was set up, the Christus bound to it with rawhide thongs— and there he was left until four that afternoon. It so happened that he lived this time; often the Christus is dead when they take him down."

"And does this still exist here in New Mexico to-day?" I asked incredulously.

"Yes, it still goes on right in San Mateo not fifty miles from the ranch. Read Charles F. Lummis's marvelous description in his fascinating book, 'The Land of Poco Tiempo.' It was he who first made known to the civilized American world the existence of these orgies. There are many curious, unknown phases of American life in this Southwest of ours, of which the Penitente brotherhood is merely the most fantastic; the cramped, meager existence of that Mormon community at Ramah is almost equally surprising in this day and age. And not only are there things bizarre and unexpected; this is even more a land of delight and enchantment: you have already

seen something of the primitive vigor of the remaining vestiges of homesteader and cow-puncher life, and also the charm of the leisurely Mexican civilization, side by side with the simplicity
and serenity of the Pueblo Indian world. Read
all of Lummis's books; he first used 'the Southwest' as a generic term, and he is high priest of
the cult. Why, there are ruins on this very towering table-rock which were old and mysterious at
the time of the fall of the Roman Empire. There
are glorious fantasies of nature which have been
in the process of formation since the beginning of
human time. Zuñi Nick, you've traveled all over
these four corner States, worked for whites, and
lived among the Navajo; what's the most wonderful thing you've ever seen?"

"Zuñi Nick think the Great Cañon. But Na-
vajo, he tell of thing he say much more great—
Nonne-zoche Not-se-lid—he call it—that mean
—Rainbow of Stone."

"Where is that, Zuñi Nick?"

"Oh, Zuñi Nick never go there—far, far—
hard on horses—no water—no food—nothing but
rock and rock."

II

THE Mormon poplars stand bare and somber, for it is still winter in New Mexico. Among the hundred barns and cabins which dot the snow-spotted valley, one huge, unpainted frame structure looms up; it is Lambson's Hall, the social center of Ramah village. A man, staggering under a load of wood, enters the hall; and soon from the single chimney rises a thin wisp of smoke.

Evening at half-past seven. The hall is dimly lighted with four antiquated lanterns, disclosing the interior of an ordinary barn without the stalls and with the addition of a floor, a stove, and a plank bench around the wall. Frank Lambson, tall, broad-shouldered, bearded, stands over the stove rubbing his hands. He wears a campaign hat, a blue shirt which is partly concealed by a mackinaw, army breeches, shoes, and puttees.

The door is flung open, and Dan Farrell, the fiddler, enters.

"Well, expect a crowd to-night, Frank?"

"Don't know. Roads are sorta bad. Don't think many'll come but us Mormons here in Ramah and a few of the Gentiles from them ranches close to town. Vogt's crowd'll probably be in; they usually ride."

"Yah, they all oughta be comin' in a little piece."

Four boys slink in edgewise and take seats on the plank bench. All affect sombreros, boots, and spurs; their shirts and ties are gaudy; their hair is slicked back. One of them chews tobacco noisily; the others smoke cigarettes. They say nothing. A little later seven girls come in together and seat themselves on the opposite side of the hall. Many of them have a fresh prettiness, but they are badly dressed and awkward. They giggle and cast sidelong glances at the boys.

Soon the door is open almost continuously to admit a steady stream of men, women, and children. Whole families are now arriving from the outlying ranches, and often three generations are represented. In attire, manner, and speech they confess the crudeness of their lives. Several couples bring their babies in baskets and stack them near the wall. All the groups divide at the door; the men go to one side of the room, the women to the other.

Half-past eight. Shrieks as from a house-cat in a coyote trap. Dan Farrell is tuning up his fiddle. He begins to play a syncopated version of the Mormon hymn, "Manna Land." The dancing is slow to begin, but several couples of the younger girls dance together, and at length four boys walk self-consciously across the hall and present themselves to four young women who are sitting together.

"May I have the next set?" they ask.

Half-past ten. The floor is crowded; the favorite steps are the "tickle-toe two-step," the Varsuvien, the Shadish. The music stops, and Frank Lambson collects fifty cents from each of the men and boys. When all have paid, the fiddler plays again, and Frank calls a circular two-step: "All join hands! Circle to the left! Grand right and left! Everybody two-step! Girls on the north side, gents on the south; forward, march; Gents, swing your girls to the right! Everybody dance!" It is strenuous business, but grandparents vie with their descendants in the energy put into the various figures.

While I was dancing with Sally Davis, the door at the end of the hall was thrown open, and two travel-worn young men rushed in shouting greetings to every one.

"Why," said Sally stopping shortly, "it's Dick Bloomfield and Sam Bond; they must 'a' just got back from Utah; they been there more nor a year." Taking my arm, she dragged me to the crying, gesticulating group, worked our way through them, and took complete possession of the returned native sons. Them and me she led to seats beside her.

"He," jerking her thumb toward me, "he's been out to Vogt's ranch for five months; he used to go to college down East, but he got sick and had to quit and come out here; he's sure a lot better now."

Bloomfield and Bond looked at me; Bloomfield seemed strong and hard, but there was a bit of fire in his eye; Sam Bond was obviously naught but Dick's silent satellite. Then Bloomfield spoke:

"Well, I don't see what he wanted to come to a place forty miles from a railroad fur. New Mexico ain't no country anyway. You oughta go to Utah. There's something to see there."

"Oh, yah, Dick, Salt Lake and the temple and . . ."

"Naw, I don't mean them things, Sally. I mean the mountains and things in that wild country around Mexican Hat where I been workin'. There's every sort of thing you never seen before there. There's just one thing I missed, but I tell you I'm goin' back for that."

"What's that, Dick?"

"That's what they call the Rainbow Natural Bridge. It's a great big bridge of stone higher than the temple, and they say there's every color of the rainbow in it. Ain't nobody hardly 'cept Indians that's ever seen it, and you can't get them to go back there most usually."

"How far is it from here?" I asked.

"It ain't more nor three hundred miles straight up northwest of here."

"We could drive up in a couple of days, then?"

"Drive up! Say, you can't get within a hundred miles of that even with a wagon! It's all horseback over worser trails than you ever see. Why, you go over rock and rock and rock for three days, and you don't see no living soul the whole pack. They say it's just like you're on a different earth."

"Well, did you have a good time?" asked Evon, as he and Shirley, his wife, and Betty, Katherine, and I galloped home.

"You bet!" I replied, but I was thinking of something else, and presently I asked him:

"Evon, do you know anything about a Rainbow Bridge somewhere in Utah?"

"Why, yes, I do know something. That's what Zuñi Nick was talking about the other night, I believe. It is said to be the most marvelous natural wonder on this continent, but it is practically inaccessible. Wetherill, the trader up at Kayenta on the Navajo Reservation, discovered it about ten or fifteen years ago, and he does take parties in sometimes."

"Believe me, I'd certainly like to get there!"

"Maybe sometime you can someway. Of course, you couldn't go now; you don't know enough about horses or traveling with a pack outfit, but I've been wondering for quite a while if it wouldn't be a good idea for you to get a couple horses and start out camping across the country a bit. It's getting a little tiresome around here, and there's lots and lots of things you want to see before you go back East. The only thing is you wouldn't want to go alone. Maybe one of your Princeton chums could come out in June?"

III

BRONCO-BREAKING

WELL, that's a fine lookin' broom-tail bronc you got there!"

"What do you really think of him, Tom? Does he look all right? Do you think he'll stand up on a long trip?"

"Maybe so. He ain't very big, and I never did like bay horses, but maybe he's all right. But he looks like a three-year-old. How old did Hatley say he was?"

"Four. He's been running on open range in the mountains ever since he was foaled."

"What did Hatley soak you fur him?"

"Thirty dollars."

"Did you have any trouble getting him?"

"Did we ever? Sam and Mr. Hatley and I located him with that herd up by Ojo Bonito about nine this morning, and what a chase he led us! Through the thickest underbrush and timber, up and down every gully. And when we

17

finally did corner him and rope him, tired as he must have been, he kicked and bit and reared around. We had a terrible time trying to lead him down off the mountain. We had to drive him mostly and pull him with the lead-rope too."

"You're goin' to 'top him off' right away like you said, aren't you?"

"No, don't believe so, Tom. I've decided to keep him in the corral, and 'gentle' him some first."

"I thought maybe so you would."

A week later I had taught my horse to eat grain by mixing oats with his alfalfa; I had allowed no one else to lead him to water; I had gradually accustomed him to the presence of the saddle on his back; he had come to seem quite docile. And so when Evon, Tom, and other punchers came in late one afternoon after riding the fence-line and suggested that it was high time for me to ride, I quite willingly saddled him, and, blissfully ignorant of the purport of the meaningful smiles of those about me, I led him from the corral and prepared to mount him for the first time.

When I put my foot in the stirrup, he reared

back on his hind legs and snorted! I readily consented that he be blindfolded and his ears held until I should be safely settled down into the saddle. Immediately the blindfold was removed, I felt that queer twitching in his back which I came to know expressed for the horse what the bark does for the dog or the buzz for the bee. He quivered, but still he hesitated. Incited by the punchers, I dug my spurs into his flanks. Two steps—a jump—my hat is off. A whirl and another jump; I almost lose a stirrup. He rears back on his hind legs, whirls, and comes down stiff-legged on his front legs; I have lost a stirrup. A series of rapid repetitions of this movement. Numerous directions from the cow-punchers:

"Hold his head up!"

"Give him his head!"

"Clamp your knees!"

"Get your stirrup!"

"Give 'im hell!"

All of which I tried to obey at once with the result that at jump six (Tom's count) I sailed over my horse's head and found myself sitting solidly on the ground, while the horse, rejoicing in regained freedom, careered wildly down the road to the accompaniment of loud shouts of laughter from the punchers and screams from Betty and Katherine.

This was all rather unpleasant; but I had been puzzling over a suitable name for my steed, unable to choose between Rex, Lightning, and Duke, and it did solve that problem, for now there was suggested one word, rich in connotation, from my meager Spanish vocabulary, which so perfectly described the manner in which my horse rid himself of me that thenceforth he was— Pronto.

With great efficiency and monotonous regularity, Pronto threw me every morning for a week. They have a proverb in the West: "A puncher can be thrown in a haystack, and he'll break his neck; a tenderfoot gets thrown off a cliff, and he bounces up smiling." So it seemed. I was catapulted against a pine-tree, rolled off in a stream, was neatly spilled over a high brush fence, fell off upon a pile of rocks, but I was hardly scratched. Gradually I became familiar with the motions of the horse's body; I grew to know what contortions to expect next and to adjust myself accordingly. I soon found that by grasping the saddle-horn tightly with one hand and holding the reins with the other I could stick to the writhing, twisting thing under me. At least some part of me was on some part of him some part of the time, although I was violating all Western ethics by thus "pulling leather."

At the end of two weeks Pronto was a very badly trained horse. He no longer pitched "high, wide, and crooked" every morning; but he was stubborn, restive, and anything but bridle-wise.

Then came a memorable spring day. I was on the porch of the ranch-house, fondly arranging cooking utensils, saddles and bridles, ropes, pack, sacks, and my glaringly new and white tarpaulin tent, when Evon joined me.

"Everything's about ready for the great adventure, isn't it? How's your other horse—the one you got from Hamblin's?"

"Tony? Oh, he's O.K. Grant Hamblin said he was 'as gentle as a cat.' "

"You're all set, then, except some one to go with you, aren't you?"

"I've about decided that I might as well start out alone. I had a letter from my last real prospect this morning, and his folks won't let him

come. So I think I might as well take advantage
of these spring days and not wait until school is
out to start. Maybe I can pick somebody else up
on the trail, or perhaps one of my friends can
join me later. Do you think that'll work out all
right?"

"It will be all right if you don't mind traveling
alone. That is, all right as long as you don't go
too far from the beaten path. Of course, you
can't think of going to the Navajo Reservation
or the Rainbow Bridge country alone. What I
think you had better do is go from here over the
Zuñi Mountains, and then take the automobile
trail to Santa Fé. That's the place where you're
most likely to be able to pick up a partner, and
you can see lots of interesting country on the
way."

"Sounds good. I think I might as well start in
the morning."

"But there's one thing yet. You'll want to al-
ternate your two horses as pack-animals, and
Pronto has never had a pack-saddle or pack on.
He may not make any fuss, but we'd better try
him. Suppose you go down and get him right
away; bring him up here, and we'll pack him."

I held Pronto at the end of a rope, while Evon packed him. When the pack-saddle was put on, he but looked at it curiously and stamped his hoofs, although a long stick was necessary to lift his tail for the breeching. Of the large white pack-sacks which were hung on the bars of the saddle, he was somewhat suspicious, yet not resentful. The roll of bedding in the canvas made him snort, and when the tying-on process began it was too much. He bolted, and our confined efforts were insufficient to hold him. Off went he, and in like manner off went bedding, tent, poles, and ax. This added to his terror.

In a moment he was but a white streak against the timber of the table-land across the valley, and I was on Tony to follow him. It seemed as hopeless as chasing greased lightning. Just as I was across the valley, my McClellan saddle, which in my haste I had neglected to cinch properly, slipped off, and I slipped off with it. Horseless, I began the hot walk back to the ranch.

There I beheld a spectacle: out in the horse-pasture all of Evon's staid work-horses running like mad, and leading the vanguard a ghostly white apparition—my Pronto—while far to the rear but gaining ground with every stride—Tony. Red, an ancient work-horse, which I had never known to step out of a decorous walk, took the wire-fence as gracefully as an English filly.

IV

THE little group who had gathered to see me off were none too sanguine. Inexperience plus a bronco horse would surely give rise to many disasters, they said. I am afraid that the way I had packed Pronto hardly induced any extreme confidence in my ability: the pack was bulky, top-heavy, and untidy, and it swayed threateningly. A pair of hobbles, forgotten until the last moment, dangled from the bed-rope; there were dish-rags stuck between the folds of the tent.

With a great deal of advice on divers subjects ringing in my ears, I took the well traveled wagon-road which fifteen minutes later brought me into Ramah. At the trading-store I loaded up on flour, bacon, various canned goods for myself, and oats for the horses. Out of the village, I passed the fertile fields of the Ramah valley, and along the base of the sheer cliffs of blood-red sandstone that rises from the shores of inviting Ramah Lake. It was a long trek across the parched plains that lay between the lake and the Zuñi Mountains. Pronto kept up well; a little too well, I thought. Four miles out I tied him to a scrub-cedar just in time; the pack needed attention.

Shortly after noon I caught my first glimpse of Inscription Rock, named by Lummis, now officially known as El Morro National Monument. My anxiety, which had hitherto rendered me oblivious to the face of the country, gave way to a keen feeling of delight on perceiving its majestic fortress-like outlines. Another mile of traveling revealed a large mesa or flat-topped hill with a precipitous eastern wall which seemed in sharp contrast to the timber-covered, gently sloping western side. I tied my horses in the shadow of the walls.

A veritable stone autograph album is El Morro. Hundreds, perhaps thousands, of years ago prehistoric visitors carved pictographs in the soft sandstone, and there they remain—enigmas as to date, meaning, and authorship; much later the rock became established as a regular stop-

ping-place on the trail between the pueblos of
Zuñi and Acoma, and passing *conquistadores* and
padres left inscriptions which suggest a whole
world of daring and adventure, of hardship and
suffering. Let some of these speak:

PASÓ POR AQUI EL ADELANTADO DON JUAN DE OÑATE AL
DESCUBRIMIENTO DE LA MAR DEL SUR A 16 DE ABRIL,
AÑO 1605.

Passed by here the Adelantado Don Juan de Oñate
to the discovery of the sea of the South, the 16th
of April, 1605.

AQUI ESTABA DE GEN. DN. DO. DE VARGAS QUIEN CON-
QUISTÓ A NEUSTRA SANTA FÉ Y A LA REAL CORONA
TODO EL NUEVO MEXICO A SU COSTA, AÑO DE 1692.

Here was General Don Diego de Vargas, who con-
quered for our Holy Faith and for the Royal
Crown all New Mexico at his own expense in the
year of 1692.

SOY DE MANO DE FELIPE DE ARELLANO A 6 DE SETIEM-
BRE SOLDADO.

I am from the hand of Felipe de Arellano, on the
16th of September, soldier.

SE PASSARON A 23 DE MARZO DE 1632 AÑOS A LA VEN-
GANZA DE MUERTO DEL PADRE LETRADO.

They passed on the 23rd of March, 1632, to the
avenging of the murder of Father Letrado.

AÑO DE 1716 A LOS 26 DE AGOSTO PASÓ POR AQUI DON
FELIZ MARTINEZ GOVERN. Y CAP. GEN. DE ESTE
REGNO A LA REDUCZION Y CONQTA. DE MOQUI Y EN
COMPAÑIA EL RDO. P. F. ANTONIO CAMANGO CUS-
TODIO Y JUEZ ECLESIASTICO.

Year 1716, on the 26th of August, passed by here
  Don Feliz Martínez, Governor and Captain-Gen-
  eral of this kingdom, to the subjection and con-
  quest of Moqui; and in his company Reverend
  Father Fray Antonio Comango, Custodian and
  Judge Ecclesiastic.

DIA 28 DE SEPT. DE 1727 AÑOS LLEGÓ AQUI EL ILLMO.
SR. DR. DN. MRN. DE ELIZAECOCHER OBPO. DE DU-
RANGO Y EL DIA 29 PASÓ A ZUÑI.

Day 28th of September of 1727, reached here the
  most illustrious Señor Doctor Don Martin de
  Elizaecocher, Bishop of Durango, and the 29th
  day he went on to Zuñi.

The last inscription of historical interest is that
of Lieutenant Simpson, U.S.A., and R. H.
Kern, the artist, who visited El Morro on a government mission in 1846. (The many Juan Fe-
lipes and Luis Jesus Manos Diazos who in recent
years have taken great pains to carve their names
for posterity, even if they had to obliterate inscriptions of historical value, would perhaps dis-
pute this last statement.) The rock is now a Na-

tional Monument, and, under the intelligent and ever-zealous custodianship of Evon Vogt, the inscriptions have been carefully translated and guarded, and the site has been made attractive to visitors.

For an hour we traversed the open sage flats, and thence moved up José Pina Cañon. The cañon is a thing of beauty indeed from its verdant flowered floor all the way up the walls, where the red and the white of the sandstone blend so perfectly. At the mouth of the cañon a vast meadow-like space stretches out toward the mountains. The gray-green sward is splotched with red islands of rock strangely wind-sculptured, rising hundreds of feet above the flat.

All too soon the shadows creeping across the mountains warned me that it would soon be night. I had yet some miles to cover if I was to reach a certain ranch, so that I could have the satisfaction of placing a fence between Tony and Pronto and the home ranch. Presently I came upon some straggling Mexican adobe houses. In the door of one of them was a pleasant Mexican woman, who assured me that *el camino à la casa de Tom Palmer* was *este*.

It was twilight when I perceived a light not more than half a mile away, which I knew must come from the ranch that was my goal, and I was congratulating myself that my first day had passed without an accident. At that precise moment a jack-rabbit jumped across the trail. The lead-rope was almost jerked from my hands, betokening that Pronto had lost his thin veneer of civilized habits and had become again a twisting, pitching, plunging, rearing thing. And then Tony—Tony whom I had bought because he was described as being "gentle as a cat"—Tony began to buck. In half a second I decided that I must loose one horse or the other. Never did I think of dismounting and holding both of them. I dropped the lead-rope, and Pronto tore off through the timber. Tony showed a disposition to run after him, but after something of a struggle became quiet. Then I hurried to find Pronto, who by this time was out of hearing.

Until it became entirely dark the trail was plain enough, for the pack had become dislodged. A tent here—blanket there—farther on a can of soup. So was I led on and on into the forest. Eventually came darkness and the realization that I was hopelessly lost. I spent a dismal night, leaning against a pine-tree, clutching Tony's bridle in my hands. As soon as it became light in the morning, I began to try to find my way to the trail; but almost immediately I heard welcome hoof-beats, and soon I was telling my story to a homesteader who proved to be a true good Samaritan. He abandoned his hunt for a lost cow, and assisted me in my search for Pronto. At last we came upon the scarcely recognizable frame of the pack-saddle. Then the stranger took up Pronto's tracks, and we followed them all morning. He had gone more than ten miles at a run! About noon we found a very tired, tractable little horse standing motionless under a cedar-tree.

The next task was to return to the scene of the night's debacle and retrieve what remained of my outfit. An ax here—here a can of beans—here a letter. By the time we had mended things and packed, it was already late, but I felt I must get on a few miles, and so after vainly trying to express my gratitude to my preserver, I began the climb up the mountain.

At the ranch which had been my objective the night before I received directions somewhat in this wise: "Follow this road for a mile or two, turn off at the first trail by a big tree to the left, when the trail forks take the one most traveled, follow it until you come to a big rock, then turn to your right, then to your left, then keep to the right in your general direction."

As the sun was sinking, I found myself on no trail at all, but in luxuriant grass on the banks of a clear, cold mountain stream. I had had a plenty of traveling in the semi-darkness the night before; therefore I unpacked and made camp immediately. I hobbled Pronto by tying his two front feet together so that he could move about to graze but supposedly could not go far; Tony I tied to a stout log. Soon the simmering of the bacon on the fire, the rhythmical murmuring of the brook, and the regular munching of the horses caused life to assume again a cheerful and calm aspect; I was very tired and, immediately after eating, made my bed upon two sheep-pelts and two Navajo saddle-blankets, and went to sleep to dream of bucking horses and of a long and beautiful trail with a rainbow at the end of it. In the morning breakfast consisted of beans tumbled out of a can, for I was eager to find a trail at once. Without incident, for Pronto was tired, we attained the top of the crater of an extinct volcano, and from there I could see a cluster of adobe houses in a valley below. I made off in that direction, and by ten o'clock I was interrogating a young Spaniard:

"Donde está el camino a Grantes?" (Where is the road to Grants?)

"Está el camino—à la mano izquierda—valle largo; Grantes—esta dirección—" and so forth at a speed beyond my following.

"No sabe," was all I could muster.

"Perhaps we had better speak English."

In a short time I was on the road to Grants, and a beautiful road it proved. It led through parks of yellow pine, past little cañons where the aspen shook. Here and there were clumps of spruce and juniper. For at least five miles the road followed a gloomy lava-bed five feet high, in which I discovered every sort of attraction— craters, ruins, and even ice-caves.

When the road forked four ways, I flipped a coin and started down the wrong fork, which brought me to a little out-of-the-way ranch. I refused the hospitable invitation to remain for the night; but, misinterpreting directions as usual, at five o'clock I was at a Mexican ranch and as far from Grants as ever. No one would have dreamed of addressing in English the *señora* who answered my knock; so again I tried my feeble Spanish. She laughed and said, "Excuse me, but if you were not so green I could put you on the road very quickly; but as it is you had better go back to Brady's and let them direct you again."

Things went better on the following day: by noon I was at the head of Zuñi Cañon, drinking the fine water which flows from ice-cold springs in the lava-beds. When I had gone a little way into Zuñi Cañon, I rejoiced exceedingly, for, after one glance at its high sheer walls where the eagles screamed from lofty aeries, I realized that I could not possibly get out of my course even if I wished to do so. At the mouth of the cañon the scattered group of frame buildings which is known as Grants, New Mexico, was discernible. A little later I had my camp pitched close to the center of the city by the side of a pleasing lagoon, in which I enjoyed a moonlight swim with some Mexican youngsters.

Before sunrise I awoke to find my horses gone.

Tony, whom I had tied to a stake, had pulled it up, and Pronto, hobbled, had followed him. (Pronto always maintained toward Tony a sort of "Where thou goest, Caius, go I also, Caia," relation.) Having spent some futile hours following the multitudinous horse-trails, I remembered the homing instinct of the animals and decided to get another horse and back-trail. After considerable parleying I secured an old work-mare known as Bonita. A few hours later Bonita and I located Tony and Pronto in Zuñi Cañon, peacefully working their way homeward.

That night I tied Tony to a tree.

V

FROM the dim wagon-roads of the Zuñi Mountains to the well marked highway between Grants and Albuquerque was an abrupt transition. My time was largely occupied in dodging the hundreds of cars full of tourists, rushing through New Mexico, never dreaming that in the land of "sun, silence, and adobe" (Lummis again!) there is more of history, more of archæology, more of human interest, and more of varied beauty than in all California. Thus in the automobile journey of one day between Albuquerque and Grants one comes into contact with three distinct and separate civilizations: the Mexican, the Indian, the modern. As to the beauty, it is there—mountain and cañon, lake and river, forest and desert. One can, however, hardly blame the tourist for doubting the beauty of New Mexico after seeing it only from the Old Trails

Highway. Less inspiring scenery than that between Albuquerque and Grants can hardly be
imagined, a dull gray, unbroken save by the irrigated farms close to the Mexican and Indian
villages, and with no vegetation but snake-weed
and occasional cactus.

After leaving Grants it was nearly a day's ríde
before I came to San Fidel and Cubero, Mexican
villages composed of one-story huts constructed
of sun-baked clay or adobe, heated by fireplaces;
the main room is usually graced by the only bedstead and adorned with colored lithographs and
family portraits. The single industry is agricul-
ture; the owner of each adobe dwelling usually
possesses a tiny farm, a *ranchito,* upon which he
grazes goats and sheep or raises beans and *chile,*
corn and squash. The life is simple and kindly,
sleepy and quaint; even the casual visitor feels
that he is tired in the land of *mañana*—to-morrow.

Some miles beyond Cubero, I left the highway
to go eastward toward the pueblo or Indian village of Acoma. From the high hill which lies between Acoma and the railroad, the panorama is
still gray, but it is now a gray sea broken by white

islands—lofty mesas of varied contour raising their sheer walls skyward. On the top of one of these is the cloud-swept citadel of Acoma.

Acoma has been described as "a city on an island in the sky." And so it seems as you first view it—an unstable ethereal thing in the heavens —more of a mirage than a reality. Leaving Tony and Pronto below, I climbed the old, old trail whose steps are cut in solid rock. In the city above, I roamed the streets between terraced adobe houses for some time; admired the Franciscan mission built in 1629 from materials entirely back-borne from the plain below; climbed to the belfry and was rewarded by observing an ancient Spanish inscription proclaiming that the bell had been cast in Seville, Spain, in 1703. Surrounding the church is the graveyard, guarded by grim clay prayer-devils on the wall, where the Acomese have been laid to rest for three centuries.

As I was looking at the primitive isinglass in a window, I saw a small group of Indians approaching. I went to meet them and offered my hand to the leader, a middle-aged man who was rather a handsome figure with strong features set off by glistening black bobbed hair and by a picturesque attire which consisted of a black velvet shirt, black pantaloons, and buckskin moccasins. His wrists, neck, and fingers were ornamented with all manner of handsome silver and turquoise jewelry. His three companions were all of the other sex and equally striking in appearance, yet hardly handsome in my eyes; the same kind of hair in the same style framed heavier features, and their short squatty figures were clothed in gay, loose-fitting cotton garments. They were typical pueblo Indians of New Mexico.

The spokesman handed me a dirty sheet of paper on which was typewritten in English and Spanish a notice to the effect that visitors to the pueblo of Acoma would kindly pay a fee of one dollar and also a fee of five dollars for the privilege of taking pictures. I had no objection to paying the fees on ethical grounds, as I felt I had had my money's worth; but unfortunately for the poor Indian, the condition of my exchequer would not permit any such contributions. And so I used the always useful "No sabe." It was evidently not very convincing, for the gentleman in black began to make motions that were anything but friendly. I reflected that it was a long four hundred feet down from the edge of the cliff, and so began to edge backward toward the center of the village. Mr. Acomite wasted no more motions but grabbed my kodak and doubtless yet retains the handle as a souvenir. Recalling something I once had heard about him who fights and runs away, I began a precipitous retreat down the trail. Possibly if most of the population of the Sky City had not been away cultivating the fields, I should not have fared so well.

The following day brought me back to the highway, and by noon I had gained the more friendly pueblo of Laguna, which is perched on a high hill above the San José River. I was most hospitably treated in the city of San José de Laguna, whose citizens enjoy a reputation for cleanliness somewhat lacking among others of their Indian brethren. Laguna is truly beautiful as well as picturesque; the homes are either painted white or tinted pink or blue; it was good to enter them at will to admire the low-raftered ceilings, the white fireplaces, the hard-packed dirt floors, the gaily ornamented pottery which served so many ornamental and useful purposes; I regretted that in some cases the effect was spoiled by cheap modern furniture.

It was well worth while to lounge on a high rock to watch a woman rhythmically grinding corn, a man shaping pottery with deft fingers, a gaudily dressed young girl coming back from the river, balancing her *olla,* or water-jar, on her head, happily singing:

I-o-ho, wonder water,
I-o-ho, wonder water,
Life anew to him who drinks!
Look where the southeast clouds are bringing rain!
Look where the southwest clouds are bringing rain!
Life anew to him who drinks!
I-o-ho, wonder water,
I-o-ho, wonder water,
Life anew to him who drinks! [1]

How well all this harmonized with the surroundings! The pueblo Indian does not dominate his environment; he belongs to it; he blends with the adobe, the turquoise skies, the sunshine, the distant mesas.

Late that afternoon I sat on the door-step with my host, a young Indian school graduate who spoke perfect English. We took a census of ten

[1] The translation is by Natalie Curtis.

tourist automobiles that passed through the village. Eight rushed by one of the most interesting sights in America at full speed. The ninth slowed down a little—they were curious at least—a man glanced around, remarked, "Another one of those damn Mexican towns," and the car passed on. No. 10 stopped, as they were in need of water. Mama glanced around, while papa got the water. She thought it was "so interesting."

Two dull days were spent in covering dull, uninteresting forty-three miles between Laguna and Los Lunas. Tony furnished the only enlivening incidents. On one occasion he lay down as I was watering him in the Rio Puerco, which, by the way, earns the epithet of *puerco,* dirty; I should not have minded had I not been on his back. He also developed the playful habit of doing his best to kick the saddle off whenever I left him tied.

I never can forget what a thrill my first sight of Los Lunas and the Rio Grande valley gave me. I had almost forgotten there was so much green on earth. Los Lunas more than fulfilled its promise from a distance; it is a truly delightful little city with beautiful trees, well kept lawns, and fine gardens adorning modern homes, but it pains me to add that I can never forgive Los Lunas for its immense bloodthirsty mosquitoes.

It was a pleasure to travel up the verdant Rio Grande valley toward Albuquerque through small Mexican villages, very quaint, and past prosperous farms. And then there was Isleta. Isleta is not so beautiful as Laguna, nor so picturesque as peerless Acoma; but the quaint irregularity of the narrow winding streets and the unexpected lines of the dwellings charm you, and the old mission church has a marvelous altar and a good ghost legend which tells how Fray Diego's coffin every hundred years pushes its way up through the floor of the church. Isleta is the largest of the Rio Grande pueblos, and her people are more prosperous than those of many of her sister villages.

San Felipe de Albuquerque, the commercial capital of the State, is a modern town, strangely bustling for the Land of Poco Tiempo, the land of "pretty soon" (again Lummis!). I remained there two days, nominally to rest my horses, really to gain a respite from my own cooking.

VI

A FTER a little difficulty, I succeeded in getting my cavalcade through the business part of Albuquerque to the road that leads northward toward the city of Holy Faith. Once thereon, I slowed my horses down to a walk, that I might better enjoy the sights along the road and on it. For it was Saturday, and it seemed that all the countryside was going to the city to market. The Mexican wagons were so loaded down with human burden that one was inclined to wonder where they would put their purchases. All were very friendly, responding with wide grins to my "Buenos días" and perchance countering with "Donde viene?" where do you come from? There were other wagons whose occupants contrasted sharply by reason of their colorful attire with the Mexicans, who were almost entirely in somber black. These were the pueblo Indians coming from Sandia and their

44

settlements on the Rio Grande—Santo Domingo, San Felipe, and Cochiti.

A knight of the road, bumming his way toward Chicago, accosted me, and we held an extended discourse on the merits of our modes of traveling. We were thus engrossed when interrupted by a cheery, "Where bound, partner?" Looking up, I was amazed to see that here was what I had hoped for but despaired of ever finding—another traveling on horseback.

"Why, I'm headed for Santa Fé and Taos right now. You're going west, I take it?"

"Well, yes. I expect to end up at the Grand Cañon eventually, and I am following the highway for want of a better way to go."

"That's funny. The Grand Cañon is my final goal also, but I intended to make a circle up through the northern pueblo district and perhaps across the Navajo Reservation first."

"You know, I'd like to see that Navajo country, too. I've heard some scarcely believable tales about its primitiveness and its beauty. If you are not in too great a hurry, what do you say if we camp right here to-night and compare notes on our travel experiences?"

After we had gone through the routine of attending to our horses and making camp, we sat by the camp-fire and listened to each other's stories. Here is Anderson's as he told it to me:

I felt stifled in New York City. Novels, movies, catalogues, lithographed calendars, visiting Europeans, Los Angelesians, Ford agents, all told me that the Wool was gradually being plucked from the West! Somehow the fact that my little grandchildren would find but few thrills in my "No battles," "No skirmishes," "No wounds" war record made me determined to spare them the humiliation of having a range-illiterate granddad. And so I betook myself to Tulsa, that Oklahoma vestibule of the old West. And there on a Saturday morning I acquired at an auction Bill, a horse (a gentleman horse, brown—age, habits, mileage, and carbureter mixture unknown). The following day I assumed carelessly a suit of outdoor clothes, took a trolley to the other end of the city, where Bill was temporarily quartered, and slowly, fearfully, and awkwardly rode once around the block. That was all. The next day: two blocks! The third day: half a mile!

The problem was to sit easily in the saddle with careless gesture; not to bounce when passing natives; haughtily to endure glances from Michigan, Massachusetts, and Montreal machines. I liked the horsy smell which remained with me wherever I went, the clunk of the old army boots on pavement and floor, the slightly diminishing belt-line.

At the end of two weeks, alone and innocent, my little-change wardrobe tied behind the saddle, I started. For me the West began as soon as I left Tulsa on that bright, though cold, March morning. It was a wire-enclosed highway, of course; but the city is left behind, the hills sweep away, the ground is primitive, my horse is alive— not a thing of gears and shifts. My first small town: porches, gates, electric-light-bulb streetlamps, children rolling in clover, hammocks, frame stores, blacksmithy, soda-parlor, jelly-beans, boarding-houses, the slam of wooden gate and a mother's "OO-HOO! Tom—mee!" The revelation of Bill's personality and all the little experiences of unsaddling under watching eyes, supervising his grub, brushing him down, were thrilling.

I made a leisurely progress by twenty-mile stages across Oklahoma, once teeming with buffalo and Indian; but now, alas, my progress was down fenced highways, forever trailing the speeding motors, drifting by neat farms, poultry ranches, granaries, oil-fields. In Oklahoma City I had a rather foolish feeling as I trotted slowly through a typical American residential quarter, passing typical people in typical garb and conveyances.

At Texola, near the Texas border, the sagebrush, the soap-plant, the bear-grass, the sandbrush, gave me the longed-for sense of actually being in the romantic West. And my supper host, a horse-doctor, remorseful over past deeds at gaming-table, bunk-house, and bar, he too had the flavor of the West. I still chuckle to remember his admonition to one of his hens, "Come, now, Miz Wartlegs, you ain't laid no aig in nary a month." I slept with Bill. Curious to know his habits, I watched the heavens through the arch of his belly and marveled at his munching, crunching, sneezing, stamping, sighing, leg-shifting, halter-yanking.

Not long after entering Texas, I met a Cherokee Indian driving a wagon. "Go on over to the ranch and make yourself at home; that's what everybody else does," was his open invitation.

"Ranch?" I queried.

"Yes, you'll soon leave these farms now." It was a transition quite remarkable: in place of plots of cultivated land on level ground, the road quite suddenly mounted a tiny hill; then this somewhat monotonous floor of farming land dropped into a cañon. I noticed for the first time several varieties of Western "hands-off," back-biting, hothouse-blossoms: prickly pear, mesquite, cactus, and turpentine- or broom-weed. No longer did wire divide man's possessions; now it was a mosaic red earth, yellow broom-weed, green grass-plots, white dusty road, purple hill shadows, golden sunlight, and silvery rails searing brown hills. Now I passed a tiny section-house and a waving Mexican woman, detoured through a side gate into desolate bottoms, and suddenly found before me a collection of neat ranch-buildings. I greeted a sweet little miss of six. "My name's Dogee [in the West, a forlorn little calf]; what's yours?"

"Mine is Jum-Sum-King-A-Low-Hit-Kee-Sow-Ging." Giggles.

"And your horse?"

"Oh, I call him John-John." She dragged me to the house, where her pleasant father invited me to stay for the night. Thereupon I made myself useful in chores and in entertaining Dogee, who insisted upon my jumping a fence, riding her saddle over the edge of a bedstead in the bunk-house, carrying her puppy and pet lamb up on the porch. Supper over and the dishes washed, we went out to the bunk-house for sleep. The next morning I was on the road again, and soon I had cut across the Texas Panhandle and was in New Mexico.

In Montoya, a tiny town at the intersection of three angular mesas, I localized myself for three-odd months. I enjoyed the contact with these rugged, kindly people and lived as one of them, waiting meanwhile for the weather to moderate a bit before crossing New Mexico. I cultivated, plowed, milked, chopped, gardened, herded, dug post-holes, chased mules, dehorned calves, doctored cows, fed and watered the entire ranch live stock, built tanks of earth to catch the rain-water, washed and wiped dishes, stretched a barbed wire, washed my own clotches, hitched and unhitched teams, shelled corn, peeled potatoes, built pig-pens, planted cotton and watermelons, irrigated gardens, rounded up cattle, branded calves, killed rattlers, trailed missing stock, learned Mexican, attended Sunday afternoon "sings," chawed to-bacco, memorized cowboy ditties, rose at dawn, slept at nightfall, ate always and everything. When I departed from my temporary home I had exchanged travel-worn Bill for my present horse, Dutch, a tough, energetic little bay. She jogs. She neither fox-trots [indicates walking with the fore feet and barely trotting with the rear, an exceedingly easy gait], paces, lopes, nor gallops! But she's tough and prairie bred.

My arrival at Santa Fé marked the completion of eight hundred miles of riding! Impressions of Santa Fé: Penitentiary smoke-stack, church spires, tall trees, expensive bungalows; then an old barn, a gully, fair equestriennes who eye me amusedly; adobe dwellings—simple or made to order with modern embellishments; now old resi-dences in deep parks, a trickling shady stream, corn-patches, a flivver, morning-glories, narrow

alley; a sense of old Orléans from the plaza, the
cathedral, the palace of the governors; the art
museum, a hotel, the post-office, and a large garage all fashioned on pueblo style; "Let us pull
adobily together" seems to be the watchword of
the Boosters; well dressed dark-skinned youth
predominating over well dressed, white-skinned
youth; tourists—gazing, pushing, talking, garag-
ing, jotting, mailing, departing. No stables!
This is the end of the old Santa Fé Trail: filling-
stations, knickers, shady trees, and white slippers,
Vandyke beards, sketching-boards, rotund Mexican politicians, curio-shops, teeming drug-
stores, legislative buildings, governor's residence,
a few Chinese! Since you are going to Santa Fé
from here, let me read you my log from there to
here:

The city behind is hidden; there are three different
shades of green on the peaks above; I pass an Indian
school and the gloomy gray stone penitentiary. Low
hills to the West; a rain over my distant road gives
the eastern hills the appearance of being wave-dashed.
We rest a short distance from the road, and Dutch
grazes; the effect of laughing voices, machine-carried,
on a solitary traveler seeking sleep on his bed of cedar-
branches. Night sounds of owl, dog, and coyote, a falling twig, the drone of wings, the hum of mosquitoes;

the red eye of a disappearing machine, the studded
sky and empty plains.

Now a long hill covered with a rash of stones and
coal-dust deposits, bare mesa; the road atop the plain.
Thirsty! Dutch laps up some water from a tiny wagon-
rut. Thinking of water as I had seen it: cold drops on
a champagne-bottle, a spurned glass beside a plate on
a winter's morn, the pulsing flow into a barn-yard
trough, tourists' dripping canteens. There is now a mile-
long, black-bouldered corkscrew to descend, and at the
bottom, surrounded by a few Indians selling pottery,
is a good cold stream.

A long barren plain at right angles to a shelved
pueblo; hills in the distance, no fences but nothing
worth fencing; droopy sage-brush, sand-drifts, timid
cactus, brown-tipped bear-grass—the terrific sun, then
the Rio Grande! Slowly it ripples by as if hating to
leave the luxuriant paradise formed by cottonwoods and
alfalfa-fields a few miles further along. Again a little
Mexican cluster of adobes, a railroad station, black
tank-tower, two trading-posts of two stories each.

I purchase a canteen. Santo Domingo fades slowly
out of sight behind a sandy hill. Braided and string-
wrapped hair, shell necklace, cotton shirts and trousers,
moccasins—pottery-makers. Down the sandy road, with
a protecting low mesa on my left, and the Rio Grande
far to the right. To either side of the road, corn,
alfalfa ditches, garden-plots, herds of horses, sheep,
cattle, and goats; a collection of Mexican houses on
one side of the river, and another Indian pueblo across
the muddy waters. Greeting to red man and brown

alike in the Spanish tongue! Night, with Dutch grazing in an alfalfa patch, an Indian for a host, an old Mexican couple for guests, Mexican dishes of *frijoles, carne,* and *tortillas.* Bed on the ground in front of the house, with the Indian on one side and a Mexican boy on the other. Stars and the moon, over this wondrous scene of primitive life seemingly so far from the bustle of cities, and then suddenly to have a roaring, clanking, glaring train burst through your illusions!

The highway again. Ditches, pasture, adobes, the wired-in road again, with the lovely gasoline smell, a transplanted Kansas farming town next, with a Main Street of orchards, cattails, rushes, meadow-larks, horse-high sunflowers, macadam, a grove by the river's edge, a shrinking pueblo far to the left, a bungalow crop, ice-plants, and here I am!

"Beside you," I said, "I seem the merest tenderfoot in traveling by horseback. When I saw you I certainly did not think I was beholding a New Yorker, a rising young business man and all that; I took you for some puncher changing location."

"And I paid you the same compliment. But this has been a happy meeting; it's too bad we seem to be traveling in opposite directions. Just exactly where do you plan to go from here, and how long do you expect to put in before reaching the cañon and ending your trip?"

"I had planned to go from here to Santa Fé, from there north as far as Taos, then back to Santa Fé, then go to the cliff ruins at Rito de los Frijoles by way of Buckman, and from there to Santo Domingo in time for the Corn Dance. After that my plans are quite indefinite. I have a vague idea and hope of getting as far west as Hopi in time for the famous Snake Dance. But my scheme in general is to deviate from my planned route whenever I hear of anything interesting to see or do."

"But what about the Navajo country?"

"Well, of course, that is really what I want most to see. It was because of things that I heard were there that I started on this trip. But every one tells me that it is quite out of the question to start out there alone, for there are no marked roads or trails of any sort; water is likely to be scarce; and the Navajos speak no English or Spanish. If there are two of you, there is a much better chance of getting along in case of an accident or anything of that sort."

"No, I certainly wish I might go with you. Of course—"

"Can't you? I am surely sick and tired of

traveling alone, and while we haven't known each other for the time prescribed by the best authorities, I am more than willing to take a chance if you are. If the arrangement doesn't work, we could always dissolve it."

"It sounds good, but I am afraid it would take more time than I could spare. You see I have already spent more time on this vacation than my health demanded, and if my job is to be kept for me, I shall have to be back in a couple of months. And I feel I must get to Grand Cañon, for everybody has told me it is the high spot in the West. There isn't really so much on the Navajo Reservation to see anyway, is there?"

"Have you ever heard of the Rainbow Natural Bridge?"

"Only the one in Zane Grey's book. But that exists only in his imagination, doesn't it?"

"No. It is real. It was discovered by an Indian trader in Utah just north of the Navajo Reservation. The Indians and white men from that country alike speak of it with awe. It is almost inaccessible, but Mr. Wetherill, who discovered it, sometimes takes parties in, and I hope that if I could ever find my way to his trading-post at Kayenta I could convince him that I could stand the trip and get him to take me in with him."

"That sounds like real adventure and romance. I'm strongly tempted, but—"

"Sleep on it; don't decide one way or the other until morning."

In the morning we collected our horses and had a light breakfast of fruit before either of us referred to our conversation of the night before. At last Anderson said:

"I'll tell you what I'll do. I must go in to Albuquerque to get my mail and probably send some telegrams. You go on to Santa Fé and Taos, and if developments do not absolutely forbid my doing so, I'll meet you back in Santa Fé in ten days."

And so we started down the highway in opposite directions.

VII

SUNDAY I celebrated by having dinner in a restaurant in Bernalillo. Onward I went through a beautiful country which had many small fruit ranches. That afternoon a motorist, who had tried to frighten my horses, ran into a ditch. It hurt him and his family no more than he had hurt me and my family, but I fancy he was quite as much frightened as Tony and Pronto and I had been when we saw his car swerve directly toward us.

By nightfall I was in an entirely grassless stretch; so at the Mexican town of Algodones I stopped, and after frenzied bargaining in Spanish I secured alfalfa for Tony and Pronto at an outrageous price, while I had a supper of *tortillas* and *chile con carne,* and then learned Spanish rapidly under the tutelage of the charming daughter of the house.

Scenery was rather lacking the next day, or,

better said, it was too much like the scenery between Grants and Albuquerque, of which I had
had quite enough. I must admit that here the
cacti in bloom were beautiful. The yellow bloom
of the prickly pear cactus looked much like a
waxen yellow rose, while the small flowers of the
bush cactus were warm and red and colorful, and
here and there the slender spiral of the lily-like
yucca waved in the wind. Then, too, the distant
mountain ranges hinted of things green and cool.

There was compensation for the lack of scenery
in the human interest of the day. First there was
the septuagenarian who was bicycling across the
continent. Strapped to the frame of his wheel
were a pneumatic bed and blankets, while in the
basket on the handle-bars was a small cooking-
outfit and a few supplies. He informed me that if
there were not too many hills he often rode forty
or fifty miles in a single day. Then the not-so-fair
young Gipsy who first wanted a match and ended
by wanting ten dollars. Twenty-five cents finally
satisfied her. She told me a rather disheartening
tale about two men, a big one and a little one,
who had evil designs against me, and to avert
many calamities I must go through rather a com-

plicated procedure, the most important part of which seemed to be parting with as much money as possible. She seemed rather disappointed when, in reply to her oft repeated question, "You don't hate to part with this ten dollars, do you?" I answered in the affirmative. Finally when she was no longer amusing I gave her the aforementioned twenty-five cents, and she showed her magnanimity by wishing me good luck. That night I camped in Domingo under a huge sign which announced to the world, "No Camping Allowed."

It was a long ride from Domingo to Santa Fé. But I felt better after climbing La Bajada Hill to the plateau whence can be seen the Sangre de Cristo range, at the feet of which lies Santa Fé. Homeward bound, Santo Domingo made frequent demands upon my canteen. If a list were compiled of the persons drinking from that canteen, it would be rather a long and interesting one.

My first impression of the capital city of New Mexico was one of extreme disgust, for it did not even possess a wagon-yard. And this the terminal of the old Santa Fé Trail! A fine Western city!

I therefore had to look around for a pasture. One grave lady was pleased to offer me grass pasture at these terms: *Quatro pesos, la noche, por caballo* (four dollars per horse per night). I declined with thanks. At last I discovered a gentleman who proved to be none other than the former chief of police. To one of such unquestioned honesty I was glad to trust my faithful family. He agreed to feed them all the alfalfa they could eat for a reasonable consideration, but his droll Pickwickian glances should have caused me to remember that he would be the one to determine how much they could eat. It was lucky for the horses that some spirit prompted me to investigate, for I found them half starved.

It was a long walk from the residence of my friend the erstwhile chief of police to the center of the city. Before I had gone six blocks up the narrow crooked streets lined with low adobes, I began to doubt that I was in the United States of North America. The streets were crowded with such un-American people, and never a word of English did I hear spoken. And when I reached the plaza this feeling was greatly accentuated, for it so happened that the day of my

advent in La Ciudad Real de Santa Fé de San
Francisco was Saturday, and Saturday night in
Santa Fé's plaza is surely unlike Saturday night
in any other city in these United States: Spanish
people promenading around a Spanish plaza
while a band plays Spanish music; beautiful
maidens wrapped in mantillas and attended by
watchful duennas; young men and old men;
friars and nuns; every one speaks Spanish, and
if by chance you hear a word of English it sounds
strange and out of place; the promenade is slow
and leisurely—they do not rush, these soft-voiced
descendants of the *conquistadores*.

In the morning, a cool, gentle Santa Fé morning, I attended mass in the cathedral. Memories
to be treasured—the Spanish people entering and
reverently crossing themselves with holy water,
the processional, the sweet music from the choir-
loft above, the archbishop on his throne, the priest
in flaming robes kneeling before the altar, the
robed friar delivering the sermon from a sort of
balcony.

The afternoon I spent wandering around. The
beautiful green plaza fascinated me. There you

can sit and gaze down the winding streets, or merely sit and dream. The square around the plaza is being reconstructed in the pueblo architectural motif: the new structures include a fine hotel whose towers copy those of Taos, Acoma, and Laguna; a large and well proportioned garage; the new post-office and government building; and the art museum, of which the exterior walls give a faint suggestion of the glories within. The Palace of the Governors, the oldest building of its kind in this country, needs no reconstruction to enhance its dignity and beauty. Walk a few minutes in any direction from the square, and you will be rewarded with a sight of the ancient, the beautiful, or the unusual. The cathedral; the Scottish Rite Temple; historic San Miguel Church; the oldest house in the United States, the mansion of the governor; the Capitol—all merit attention. In the Capitol you may witness the astonishing spectacle of an American legislature carrying on deliberations in Spanish, and of the highest judicial body in a State meting out justice to American citizens in an alien tongue. The curio shops, which seem to be without number, provide an endless source of delight. And the studios of the extensive art colony are well worth a visit.

On the following day I took a peep into the museums, First, the art museum, which houses many of the finest paintings of the Southwest. Then the New Mexico State Museum, located in El Palacio. From this historic building the whole Spanish Southwest was governed for more than a century; it was the seat of the American Territorial government; it was there that Lew Wallace wrote the final chapters of "Ben-Hur." Now, as is but fitting, it is the resting-place for many articles important in New Mexican history. They range with regard to time from pottery made by prehistoric inhabitants to the pen with which Taft signed the act of Congress which made New Mexico a State.

IMMEDIATELY BELOW TO-YO-A-LAN-A CASTS ITS SHADOW UPON
THE IRRIGATED GREEN VALLEY SURROUNDING ADOBE-TER-
RACED ZUÑI PUEBLO

AT THE TRADING-STORE, RAMAH, NEW MEXICO

SHEER CLIFFS OF BLOOD-RED SANDSTONE THAT RISE FROM
THE SHORES OF INVITING RAMAH LAKE

INSCRIPTION ROCK, EL MORRO NATIONAL MONUMENT

A PRECIPITOUS EASTERN WALL

A SPANISH INSCRIPTION AT EL MORRO, SUPERIMPOSED UPON A
PREHISTORIC PICTOGRAPH

PART OF THE LAGUNA PUEBLO

I ENJOYED A SWIM WITH SOME MEXICAN YOUNGSTERS

THE FRANCISCAN MISSION AT ACOMA, BUILT IN 1629

PRAYER-DEVILS ON THE WALL OF THE GRAVEYARD AT ACOMA

THE OLD MISSION CHURCH AT ISLETA

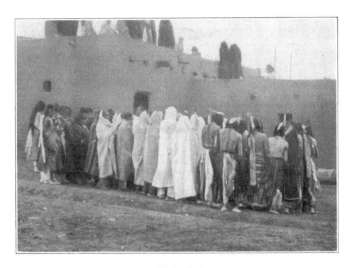

THE RAIN DANCE, TAOS

A LAGUNA GIRL BALANCING HER OLLA, OR WATER-JAR, ON
HER HEAD

THE MISSION CHURCH, EL RANCHO DE TAOS

GRADUATED FROM RIDING-TROUSERS TO CORDUROY PANTS AND
PUNCHER BOOTS

LLOYD FLETCHER, FOREMAN OF THE PANKEY RANCH

THE JEMEZ MOUNTAINS ABOVE EL RITO DE LOS FRIJOLES

THE CLIMB TO LA CUEVA PINTADA

PORTION OF THE ENTABLATURE, LA CUEVA PINTADA

THE KOSHAREE, OR DELIGHT-MAKERS

THE DANCE SETTLED DOWN IN ONE WIDE STREET

MALE DANCERS, SANTO DOMINGO CORN DANCE

THE RUINS OF AN ANCIENT PUEBLO AT AZTEC, NEW MEXICO

WONDROUS TINY VILLAGES AT MESA VERDE, COLORADO

WE HAD FORGOTTEN THAT OUR APPEARANCE BELIED ANY
SUGGESTION OF ILL HEALTH

A VALLEY OF THE UPPER JEMEZ MOUNTAINS

WE THOUGHT THE SHIPROCK A FITTING SYMBOL OF THE
SOLITUDE

TYPICAL WAGON-ROAD AND SCENERY OF THE NAVAJO RESER-
VATION

THE INDIANS WERE ALWAYS READY TO HELP US FIND OUR WAY

ROY AND JOHN AT BREAKFAST

WATERFALL, CEBOLLA CREEK, ZUÑI MOUNTAINS

NAVAJO WOMAN WITH RUG ON LOOM

THE CHILDREN TAKE THE HERDS FROM THE HOGAN

UPPER CAÑON DEL MUERTO IN THE RAIN

NAVAJOS RIDING DOWN DE CHELLY AT SUNSET

A SHEEP-HERDER IN HIS TEMPORARY SHELTER

THE WRITER AND A NAVAJO MAIDEN

SHEEP GRAZING IN THE ZUÑI MOUNTAINS

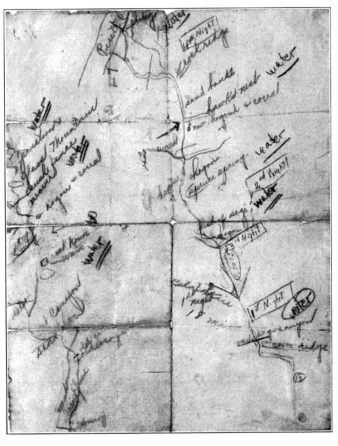

THE LITTLE MAP WHICH RED AND JACK HAD DRAWN THE
NIGHT BEFORE

NAT SIS AN . . . SYMBOLICAL OF NAVAJO NATURE

WE HAD OUR WHOLE OUTFIT OUT OF THE SEGI

AT TIMES WE TRAVELED OVER SOLID ROCK FOR HOURS AT A
STRETCH

THE WAY LED NOT THROUGH THE DOMES OR AROUND THEM
BUT OVER THEM

WE WENT ACROSS A NARROW LEDGE

DOWN INTO THIS STEEP AND NARROW DECLIVITY WE WENT

NONNE-ZOCHE NOT-SE-LID, THE INCOMPARABLE

THE RAINBOW NATURAL BRIDGE, NONNE-ZOCHE NOT-SE-LID

NAVAJOS GATHERED AT THE YEI BIΓ CHAI

WE WERE UPON TUSAYAN PLATEAU

THE SONG-PRIEST COMPLETING A NAVAJO SAND PAINTING AT THE YEI BIT CHAI

VIII

TO THE PYRAMIDS OF TAOS

THE road from Santa Fé to Taos takes the traveler through scenery that is altogether pleasing and interesting. After climbing the hills on the outskirts of the city one goes through five miles of rolling country which is covered with sparse timber. On the right is the magnificent Sangre de Cristo range; on the left, more distant, the Jemez Mountains. The first settlement encountered is the pueblo of Tesuque, which is small and not at all extraordinary. A little farther on, one comes into a series of lovely valleys where the blooming alfalfa gives a wonderful fragrance to the air. In them are countless Mexican settlements and also San Juan pueblo; this superficially seems to differ little from the Mexican towns. At Velarde the road strikes the Rio Grande and follows the Rio Grande Cañon for about fifteen miles. Here the river is totally different from the wide, placid, and muddy stream at Los Lunas, and is more like a mountain stream, its clear swift waters gushing in many rapids. At last the road emerges upon a high plateau, whence the beautiful Taos Mountains are visible.

Early one afternoon I reached Rancho de Taos, a Mexican settlement located in an exquisite valley, having as its chief glory a beautiful mission church which dates from 1778. From there it was but a few miles to San Fernando de Taos, an old-looking town, once the home of Kit Carson, now noted for its artist colony.

On hearing that the Indians of the pueblo were that day culminating a three-day rain-making labor, I hastened to stable my horses and begin the two-mile hike to Taos pueblo, the proper name of which is San Gerónimo de Taos. I hurried down a long avenue of trees which would have seemed more appropriate in a New England village than in New Mexico; the road was crowded with Mexicans in gala attire returning from the dance.

I cannot soon forget my first glimpse of Pueblo de Taos. A scene more pleasing to the eye could hardly be imagined: immediately in

front of me fields of alfalfa and waving grain
interspersed with plum thickets and Indian paint-
brush growing head-high. Perhaps a mile away
were the two pyramid-like structures which are
the communal houses of the village. Just above
them rose Pueblo Peak, snow-capped, green, and
beautiful. A close-up of the village revealed even
more of charm. For the receding brown terraces
from the first to the seventh were covered with
men and women; the men were wrapped in white
sheets, while the women wore black shawls.

As I drew near I caught the sound of the
drums and of the chanting. The Rain Dance itself was a thing of exquisite beauty; the dancers
went through slow, graceful movements in perfect rhythm with the weird yet hauntingly beautiful music which was furnished by a drum and
a chorus composed of the elders of the pueblo.
The youths who took part in the dance were more
handsome as a group than any Indians I have
seen before or since. The dark and slender
maidens partook of an Italian sort of beauty,
and the young men had fine features and trim
athletic physiques, while the costumes would have
done credit to Ziegfeld: the long black hair of

the girls was confined only by a beaded band across the forehead; their blouses and skirts were strikingly beautiful, all silks and ribbons; around their waists they wore Zuñi girdles. They were ornamented with a profusion of Navajo jewelry; the hair of the men was also loose, and they were naked to the waist unless one considers much white paint as clothing; they wore kilts of silk and calfskin moccasins. The white sheets of the old men in the chorus stood out in striking contrast to this display of color.

In the excess of my enthusiasm for the dance I became guilty of a breach of etiquette. Fearing lest it would soon be too dark, I took out my camera and, before any one knew what I was doing, I had a snap-shot of the dance. This produced a jarring note from the chorus of chanters, and for a second it appeared to me as if I had an excellent chance of being mobbed. Such a jabbering in English, Spanish, and Taos! I was confronted by the governor of the pueblo. At first things looked as if I might see the inside of the Taos jail, but finally I convinced him that I had acted in mere ignorance. I was let off with a fine.

All too soon the sun set in the azure sky, and the Rain Dance was over. The dancers retired to the kivas (sacred ceremonial chambers), and the village was given over to feasting and games. The favorite game was what is known as a chicken-pull. The rules of the sport are somewhat as follows: a chicken is placed under a rock about thirty yards in front of the participants in the game, who are all on horseback; the leader rides forward and seizes the chicken; at once the others start after him, and then it becomes a free-for-all; every one tries to get the chicken, and especially the head of the chicken; the game is continued until there is nothing whatever left of the poor fowl. The white-robed figures racing back and forth in the twilight were suggestive of Arabs.

The following day I began my return to Santa Fé to meet Anderson. The only incident worth chronicling was listening to music from Los Angeles, Denver, and Fort Worth while camped in a very lonely spot in New Mexico. I had joined a group of artists from Boston who were on a tour of the world in their motor-car, and their very complete camping equipment included a radio outfit. That was the only incident worthy of mention, but I well remember an all-day drenching rain which proved that the people of Taos had not danced and prayed in vain.

IX

THERE you are! Good! I have had to try hard these past two weeks to keep myself from hoping too strongly that you would come, and I came to this post-office rendezvous of ours this morning with many a fear in my heart."

"Well, you see I am graduated from riding-trousers to corduroy pants and puncher boots, and I'm all ready to hit the westward trail with you. When do we start and for where? That route you outlined before sounded good."

"Suppose we stick to that tentatively anyway. We'll go from here to Rito de los Frijoles, and then to Santo Domingo for the Corn Dance. I've been looking at some maps here, and I believe we would do well to hit west from Santo Domingo across the Jemez Mountains and on to Farmington, which is a small town in northwestern New Mexico and the gateway to that part of the Navajo Reservation. Now we'll have to market. Which horse shall we pack?"

"I think it would be a good idea to initiate my 'grandma horse,' Dutch, into the duties and responsibilities of a pack-animal at once."

It was noon when we paused at Agua Fría, several miles from the capital city, to eat our lunch of fruit. Between bites, we answered the questions of the Mexicans who had surrounded us. The conversation probably did not differ in two words from those at fifty other odd times when we talked with the Mexicans in that hybrid language which is so common in the Southwest:

"Donde viene?" (Where do you come from?)

"Santa Fé."

"How far you go?"

"Oh, muy lejos!" (Oh, a great distance!)

"Well, adios." (Well, good-by.)

"Adios, señores."

A little farther on we were joined by a man on horseback who introduced himself as Lloyd Fletcher, foreman of the Pankey Ranch. To use his own phrase, he was "jest a pure-D cow-puncher." Mr. Fletcher evinced considerable interest in Tony; knowing that most punchers

would rather trade horses than eat, I was not
surprised when he made me a proposition. He
suggested that Tony and my new Navajo saddle-
blanket would be a fair exchange for the white
lady he was riding, who, he said, responded to
the euphonious appellation of Daisy. As Tony
had been acting unusually foolish, I seriously dis-
cussed the trade. But before anything was settled
we arrived at Lloyd's home ranch and were· invited to spend the night in his homestead, which
adjoined the 125,000-acre Pankey Ranch.

We were soon settled in his shack, a simple
place of one room, constructed of cedar logs,
mud-plastered, and with a dirt floor. His clothes
were over a wire in one corner, a box of personal
belongings under the frame bed, a gun in a hol-
ster strapped around the head of the bed, the tiny
cook-stove in another corner, two boxes for chairs,
miscellaneous ropes, saddles, cans of provisions,
a nose-bag full of eggs, a semi-white town shirt
in a wash-basin, and lantern-spurs. This was the
puncher's home. His is a noble profession, almost
of the past, courageous, frank, devil-may-care;
the homesteaders have wired off his open ranges;
the automobile has claimed him to quicker trans-

portation; and only the occasional rodeo brings forth his skill with lasso.

I was elected to culinary honors, and I rejoiced at the opportunity to display my skill in the gentle art. The steak was excellent, but the potatoes suffered because I became too much engrossed in one of Lloyd's yarns. Roy and I had both fancied that our appetites were prodigious, but after seeing our host eat we refrained from boasting for some time.

The meal over, we swapped stories for hours. Lloyd Fletcher told us of his life from the time when he had taken his first job as a cow-hand at eleven years of age. The tale made us realize in a greater measure what a pity it is that the genus cow-puncher will soon be extinct in this country. His narratives were abundantly garnished with many expressive phrases. Of these we agreed that the most choice was, "I ain't had sech a good time since the old sow eat my brother."

In the morning Lloyd wrangled our horses while we prepared breakfast. We decided that it was essential that one of our firm at least equal our host's appetite. But when the feast was over the records stood thus:

Mr. Fletcher: eggs, 9; pancakes, 15; slices of bread,
6; oranges, 2; bananas, 3; bacon, 7 slices.

Mr. Kluckhohn (second): eggs, 7 (I tasted them for
a week thereafter); pancakes, 6; slices of bread,
0; oranges, 1; bananas, 3; bacon, 3 slices

I will not humiliate Mr. Anderson by enumerating the few items which made up his meal. Alack, too many repasts in New York's restaurants had deprived him of even the hope of a real appetite.

Possibly because he realized we were in a stupefied condition, Lloyd resumed trading talk. I told him that I must trade both of my horses or neither. I really felt that it might be advantageous for me to trade, inasmuch as both Tony and Pronto were becoming leg-weary, and I might not again have the chance to leave them in such good hands. After all was said and done, I no longer had Tony, Pronto, and $7.50, but I possessed the spinster, Daisy, and an old gentleman-horse, Henry.

Fletcher prevailed on us to remain with him another day. First we made his rounds with him; we then made a visit to the crater of an extinct volcano. As Roy remarked, the black abyss, fifty feet across, and, it seemed, an eternity deep, would have been an ideal place to dispose of a good many things.

The next morning I took a last regretful look at Tony and Pronto; then we were on our way again. That day we spent a goodly amount of time in testing our horses for any little idiosyncrasies they might possess. We agreed that Roy's horse, whose name was Duchess when she was good and Dutch when she was annoying, had an entirely negative personality. On occasion, she could be stubborn, but vicious, never. She had contributed two colts to the demand for workhorses; she was entirely surfeited with the pleasures of horse-gossiping; Romance passed her by; she desired only to eat herself into a state of coma and then protest gruntingly the entire next day at her increased load. A series of experiments, cautiously conducted, assured us that the fastidious Henry horse was not at all dangerous despite his playful habit of snorting when any one approached him. Henry was a slender sorrel with four white gaiters embellishing his aristocratic legs; his eye was cold and haughty; a bachelor to the end of his days, he merely snorted at the least disturbance, and pursued his grazing at night ever cold toward the amorous advances of the lady packhorse. Our white horse was a lady without reproach, an ideal packhorse; born of humble parentage, she had served as a grocery-store delivery-system, acquiring a pernicious habit of devouring anything, sour or sweet, liquid or solid, vegetable, fruit, candy, which came within reach of her greedy maw; keenly and properly particular about her middle she resisted every attempt to cinch her, and was forever taking playful nips at my ribs as I laced her. Her name worried us. Daisy was impossible; we had under advisement Chona, Lily, Cleopatra, and Clytemnestra; temporarily we called her Whity or Pack.

At 4 P.M. we made a triumphal entry into the city of Buckman. We stopped at a building which was a combination of principal residence and store, curio shop, depot, post-office, and tourist information bureau. There we inquired about the trail to Frijoles Cañon. It appeared that there were two routes: the one, a prosaic but safe automobile road; the other, a trail which was "bad in places." (A truer statement would have been that it was bad everywhere and worse in places.)

We took the trail, or rather attempted to take it. "We will take the trail," said Roy to the store-keeper, "because we wish to get off the beaten path." I am here to testify that we did get off the beaten trail, although now and then we found an ancient cow-path. By sundown we must have progressed at least two miles. We staked Dutch and Henry for the night, but we merely hobbled Whity, trusting that her irreproachable conscience would not permit her to wander far. During the night we heard a great deal of breaking of brush around our camp; in consequence we were thrilled by the thought of mountain lion and bear. Morning, however, revealed a peaceful herd of Herefords.

We began our trail-breaking early; for hours we plowed through dense underbrush and black, vile-smelling bogs, the trail perilously hovering over the river; the slipping, sliding, grunting horses endeavored to find secure foothold amid the rocks. A sudden climb allowed my saddle-girth to slip backward, and I suddenly found myself astride his quivering tail. Yet, as Anderson observed, the scene was wild and beautiful: the coloring effects in the deep cañon which the Rio

Grande had chiseled were brilliant and of infinite shadings; across the river, the hills towered, grassy plots above the brown ribbon; a heron flopped lazily on a drifting railroad-tie. The frequent springs and the green-fringed brooks were a joy on that hot day. At times we had to stop on account of the positive impossibility of advancing; then one of us would reconnoiter, and finally we would find a way. All morning we strained our ears to catch the sound of falling water, as we had been told that this would signal the entrance to Frijoles Cañon. We were fearing that we had passed the entrance to the cañon when one of those blessed Forest Service signs presented itself to view. It read, "El Cañon del Rito de Los Frijoles" (the Cañon of Bean Brook).

Soon we were ascending a steep but well built government trail. In folds like the coils of a serpent it wound up and down the walls of a picturesque cañon. Some of the vistas here were worth the long day of trail-finding: the cañon of the Rio Grande now miles away and a thousand feet below us; the floor of Frijoles Cañon immediately below, covered with a dense growth of

cottonwood and aspen, through which the beautiful brook picked its way; the heralded falls where
the little stream descends 160 feet in two wondrous ribbons.

Perhaps five miles from the mouth of the cañon
we descended to its floor into a fine grove of yellow pine. Up the brook we followed until we
reached a small dude ranch; this is the opprobri-
ous title bestowed by cow-men upon a tourist resort where the guides are attired in excessively
broad-brimmed hats, intensely high-heeled boots,
and unnecessary chaps, properly to awe tourists
who arrive by motor from the East. A stone's
throw from there were some of the cliff-dwellings
which have made El Rito de Los Frijoles famous.
Our first sight was the magnificent communal
house of Tyuonyi which is built level with El
Rito. Above, the ancient race had hollowed dwellings in the soft volcanic rock of the cañon walls.
What a picture it must have been a thousand
years ago: blue sky; a green-shot tumbling
brook; dense foliage of cottonwood, silver, green,
and gold; the buff of the ripening corn; the hard
orange of powdered dust trails; black the win-
dows and entering apertures against the white

wall of the huge, porous, volcanic rock formation containing the abodes of this now vanished race. The same homes, but not then in ruins; the same delightful groves, but the .whole scene teeming with life, with colorful life as in the pueblos of to-day. For some hours we wandered among the remains. Many of them have been excavated and restored by the School of American Research at Santa Fé. Here was a kiva, or underground clan chamber sacred to elaborate ceremonials. There a stone floor, where surely the population of the cañon must have danced in the moonlight. In the houses the roofs were yet black from smoke centuries old. A trail had been worn in the soft rock below the dwellings. Foot-path of the centuries!

In the glory of a sinking sun we hurried up the old trail out of the cañon and none too soon found a camp-site on the grass-covered Pajarito plateau.

The early morning ride was a revelation. I wish it could be permitted to every one who thinks New Mexico a desert to ride as we did through the Santa Fé National Forest from the upper end of Frijoles Cañon to the Rio Grande. Along the walls of the deep, mysterious cañons, spruce, juniper, pine, oak, aspen, and poplar combine to make a perfect mosaic of living green. Everywhere great trees of yellow pine shaded luxuriant grass and a variety of flowers of every color.

In the heart of the forest are the Stone Lions of Cochiti; they are surrounded by a crude stone wall. Unmistakably specimens of aboriginal sculpture, they are much smaller and less elaborately carved than I had supposed. Nevertheless it was indeed a spot to intrigue the imagination.

After we had descended from the plateau into the barren lower portion of Capulin Cañon, we visited that little known marvel, the Painted Cave. As first seen from the trail it was a barely discernible hole high up in the wall of the cañon. Closer, we could see a striking painted frieze on the wall of the cave. Directly below was a ruin; from this a perpendicular trail led upward to the cave. It was a dizzy climb of eighty feet, with nothing for support save footholds and fingerholds in the rock. But the closer examination of the entablature made it worth while. The frieze was made up of gorgeous figures painted on the wall of the cave in red, black, and yellow. The figures were mostly those of animals, including the buffalo, the crocodile, and the reindeer, while others appeared to represent deities. A thing of unfathomable mystery!

From La Cueva Pintada we made our way across country to our old friend El Rio Grande; and again we followed its sinuous curves until we arrived at the pueblo of Cochiti, which, it is believed, was founded by an emigration from Frijoles Cañon. The people of Cochiti were extremely friendly and courteous; one of them directed us to the ford in the Rio Grande. It was with some trepidation that we began the crossing of the river; we forded it without mishap, however.

It was our intention to spend the night in Santo Domingo, that we might be ready for the feast of St. Dominic on the following day, but as we were passing through the village of Peña Blanca, we were accosted by an engaging Mexican who enticed us to his home, where he offered us horse-feed for four dollars a night. We were about to hurry out, and Mr. Lee Leyva hurried after us. His price came down to a dollar and a half; we were unable to resist. It seemed a lucky chance, for Mr. Leyva assured us that he knew a short way across the Jemez Mountains. "You can't miss it," was the burden of his discourse.

X

ON August 4 the road from Peña Blanca to Santo Domingo was transformed from an ordinary dirt ribbon beside the Rio Grande into a convulsing, colorful highway. Every one was going to the Indian village to witness the paradoxical spectacle of a feast-day of the Catholic church being celebrated not only with a mass, but also with pagan ceremonies which originated centuries before the Indians had heard of St. Dominic or any other saint, and which consisted of prayers to gods of which St. Dominic had certainly never heard.

Just as we rode into the pueblo a bell began tolling the hour for mass. We entered the church. The sight which first drew our eyes was the image of the saint enthroned above the altar. On the platform were eight or nine Franciscan fathers from the near-by towns and pueblos; it was explained to us that on August 4 the Franciscan fathers take charge of the ceremonies, while on the feast-day of St. Francis the Dominican friars have the precedence. The church possessed no seats for the congregation except a bench which followed the wall, and therefore one must make a choice between standing or sitting on the dirt floor; at this time Indians, Mexicans, and Americans were standing so close together that it would have been impossible for any one to sit down. The priest celebrating the mass had for his altar-boy the governor of the pueblo, and a choir composed entirely of Santo Domingo Indians gave the responses. It sounded rather queer to hear their aboriginal voices intoning the Latin.

The mass over, a procession formed near the altar, marched down the church, out of the door, and through the streets of the village. At the head was carried a great silken standard, then followed the image of the *santos* reverently borne by two Indians, next came the priests, and lastly the whole population of the village, arrayed in its best. They were really a fine-looking group of first Americans, the men especially. Until the procession returned to the church the bell tolled incessantly.

There was a short interval in the proceedings while those who were to dance retired to the kivas to dress. (Kiva is a Hopi word which means an underground sacred ceremonial chamber. The word has been generally applied to the ceremonial rooms of all pueblos, although in many, as in Santo Domingo, the rooms are above-ground and entered from the top by means of a ladder.) The kivas in Santo Domingo are large and are circular. They are two in number; one is the kiva of the "summer people," the other that of the "winter people."

A shot! Silence. A bell tolled. From the center of the village a dull monotonous chant. A swirl of dust from a near adobe. Then from the shadows of the walls came a solid phalanx of tribal elders advancing at a shuffling gait, intoning a low weird appeal to the heavens. Their gray hair hung loosely over their shoulders; they wore cotton shirts of pink, blue, and white hanging over their cotton trousers in Chinese fashion. The huge tom-tom followed, maintaining an intense, low, feverish beating. Boom! Boom! Boom! Boom! One—two—three—four. One—two—three—four. Then an abrupt halt, a short beat, and the tempo was resumed. Followed a leader in bright red coat and trousers with brass buttons, then the prayer-flag borne aloft. Then the dancers themselves—they must have numbered at least two hundred—first a man, then a woman in one formation; then a line of men opposite a line of women. The men were undoubtedly the more picturesque figures; the regular male dancers were costumed thus: on top of their heads was fastened a knot of brilliant-colored plumage, their long, curly, black hair hung loosely over their shoulders; to the waist they were naked; in place of clothing they wore ropes of beads and necklaces of bears' teeth; their arms and hands were painted, and just below the elbow of each arm was fastened a spray of cedar; around their loins they wore cotton kilts; on their feet were moccasins of buckskin. The Kosharee, or Delight-Makers, are the priests of the summer people. Ten of them danced outside of the main line of dancers. They were grotesque clownlike figures whose naked bodies were painted a ghastly white. The women wore on their heads an elaborate object which symbolized the growing corn. Their hair also fell loosely over their nude shoulders. Much jewelry, dark skirts, and buckskin boots were the essentials of their costume.

The dance wound in and out among the crooked streets. The figures were slow yet elaborate and graceful, and in rhythm which was wonderful to behold. Several youngsters who could not have been in their teens were among the best performers. After an hour or more, the winter people in the dance withdrew to their kiva. Thereafter the winter people and the summer people danced alternately as teams. There seemed to be considerable rivalry between them. The whole ceremony is known as the Corn Dance and was formerly held to propitiate the olden gods to give rain that the corn might flourish.

The gathering was almost as bewildering as the dance itself. A dozen or more pueblos were represented; the few Navajos from their distant reservation stood apart by reason of their tall, handsome figures and their aloof, haughty bearing; countless Mexicans, enjoying the holiday as became good Catholics, held high revelry in a miniature fair at the other end of the pueblo. And there were many (too many) Americans, some of whom had come great distances to see this, a typical example of Amerindian culture. One might hear seven or eight different languages spoken at the same time. It was, however, not difficult to make one's self understood. Almost all of the older Indians spoke Spanish, and many of the younger ones spoke English.

The dance settled down in one wide street, at the head of which was the brush pavilion which had been erected for the governor and his council. But do not assume that this was a courtesy for royalty. On the contrary, Amerindian pueblos have had republican government for centuries. The governor is elected for a term of one year by a universal male suffrage. His council is made up of the *principales,* or those who have been governors, and this council is the supreme authority in the village, while the governor and the war-chief are simply the executive officers. The once important functions of the war-chief have dwindled to supervision over communal hunts and jurisdiction over boundary lines and disputes arising therefrom. Shrouded in mystery are the powers of the *caciques,* or principal priests. Their office is lifelong and hereditary; they are dedicated to a life of fasting and praying for the benefit of the village; they unquestionably exercise a large influence in deciding important questions, but the best authorities say that the *caciques* are subordinate to the council.

It was to this pavilion that we betook ourselves to obtain permission from the governor to take pictures. We were presented to his Excellency, Señor Feliciano, and a firm "No!" was his answer to our plea. The usually effective bank-notes were not potent in this case. A little later we met our friend Lee Leyva, and he offered to get permission for us, saying that he had great influence with the governor, who had often worked for him. "No, I do not wish it," was the reply of the governor this time.

Therefore we resolved to do it without permission. We were just a little startled to see a young artist from Santa Fé thrown from a roof with the shreds of his pictures—all because he had dared to sketch. That we must use great discretion became evident, and it became even more evident when a young Indian came up to tell us that the governor had decided that the penalty for taking pictures would be six months in jail.

Unfortunately we realized that he could imprison us if he wished, and our only appeal would be to the commissioner of Indian affairs at Washington.

We began to wander aimlessly around the village; we observed with interest that a certain group of Indians wandered away at the same time and in the same direction. We tried several expedients to divert their attention without avail; at last I gave Roy the case to the camera stuffed with handkerchiefs, I put the kodak under my coat, our friends followed him, while I slipped into an empty house near the dance and from a window took all the pictures I wished. Later in the day a little silver was persuasive enough to cause two young Indian dancers to pose, forgetting the edict of the governor and the customs and fears of their ancestors.

The dance ceased at sundown, and the village was given over to feasting and revelry. All hail to St. Dominic!

On our way back to Peña Blanca we had an experience which was interesting if not pleasant. We were crossing a desert-like stretch when a storm arose with true New Mexican swiftness. I had often laughed at stories of travelers lying with face to the ground during a sand-storm, but we now found that was an extremely convenient pose. I might add a few words to the time-honored formula: if you have horses hold their reins *tight*. We found that it was most disconcerting to chase a snorting, fastidious, elusive horse when the sand in the air was so thick that you could neither see, breathe, nor hear.

XI

WITH this popular bromide of the road, Lee Leyva closed his directions for finding the trail which would be a short cut across the Jemez Mountains. According to him we had merely to follow one plain wagon-road which ended at a well marked Forest Service trail, which led directly to Jemez Springs. Jauntily we rode forth from Peña Blanca. Our faith wavered a trifle when, after eleven miles, the road forked four ways, all forks leading in the same direction, and all of about the same degree of plainness. Had we had more experience on the trail we should have returned to Peña Blanca, but after considerable discussion we decided that the left-hand road must be the one we desired. It was not. After two hours of riding we came to a deserted cabin where the road terminated abruptly, and the broken nature of the country prevented us from forging on without a road. We returned to the forks. The second road we tried was of quite a different nature: it did not end at all, it seemed; branch after branch went off in every conceivable direction. The forest received us silently—no welcoming song of brook or spring.

To add to our distress, it soon appeared that Dutch was rapidly becoming ill. Night fell, and we knew not where we were and had no source of water-supply, and when we unpacked, we discovered that we had lost a canteen and therefore had only about a quart of water left. Supper was a dismal meal that night; Dutch lay groaning on the ground, and every symptom tended to show that she had been fed wheat by Señor Lee. I surmise that the ears of our erstwhile host must have tingled while we sat around the camp-fire that night.

Morning brought no relief to the sick horse; she was no worse, but traveling with her was out of the question. And so after breakfast we separated to search for water. I put Henry into a fast trot, and for hours we rode up and down cañons, through brush and timber, but never a sign of water nor of human habitation did I see.

When, after considerable difficulty, I found my way back to camp, I found Roy holding Dutch's head; she had raised her nose from the dust to lick the perspiration-soaked slimy guard. He had returned from an equally fruitless search but a few minutes before.

There was only a swallow of water left, and we resolved to save that for a positive emergency. I made chocolate of our condensed milk; unfortunately it burned, and so the cotton taste in our mouths was accentuated rather than diminished by the chocolate.

The white horse was exhausted; the flip of a coin decided that I should continue the search for water on Henry. Instead of continuing my previous system of making a circle around the camp and investigating every water-sign, this time I rode in as straight a line as the character of the country would permit. I had not been gone from camp more than an hour when by chance I saw a broken board lying on the ground at the foot of a pine-tree. Eagerly I dismounted and picked it up: "La Jara Spring, ½ mile." I could not restrain a shout. At once I began the search, but a moment later I concluded that it would be better to move our whole outfit to this spot, so that Roy and I could systematically and thoroughly search every foot of the terrain within a mile radius.

It was a task to move Dutch; she would suffer herself to be led a few steps, would halt, and with feet and jaw set would resist every effort to budge her. Her bulging eyes with the great hollows behind them and her drawn stifle were hard to bear. What a journey! We could not see the sun, but we knew from the lessening light which filtered through the matted canopy of leaves above us, and from the ever-lengthening shadows at our feet, that it was setting. But still we unwillingly spurred our horses, and on they stumbled through the trackless, trailless forest. The green cool forest of song where rippling brooks are as numerous as the trees! What a mockery! Ah, yes, there were trees, green trees; but our swollen tongues, that cotton taste in our mouths, our feverish and sweatless bodies—all these denied even hints of coolness, and the image which was evolved by the thought of brooks was agony.

When the complete blackness which immediately follows the setting of the New Mexican sun menaced us, we halted in a little cañon through which torrents of cold water from the mountain-top must surely have rushed in the springtime. We had barely spirit enough to throw the saddles and packs from the backs of our animals; and this, indeed, seemed a wasted effort on our part, for they stood motionless, regarding us reproach-fully, and refusing entirely to graze. Having built a fire for light, we let our protesting bodies sink gradually to the ground. Gone were the fruit, the canned tomatoes, everything in our packs which could even suggest relief from thirst. And so we made no attempt to eat, but continued the search for water with our flash-lights, crawl-ing about on the ground and digging with our fingers. At last we lay almost inanimate, for even a slight movement of our limbs was a torture, and to speak was unthinkable. The events and in-cidents of the past few days conflicted strangely and painfully in my thoughts with dismal grop-ings toward the future, but after an infinite time I relaxed, I know not how, into a nervous and troubled sleep. In this state I was pursued by grotesque demons, haunted by weird apparitions, and blessed by beautiful visions, which changed, with the rapidity possible only in dreams, to hideous nightmares.

Before sunrise we again started out in different directions, realizing that this time we must find water before nightfall. I must have ridden for three hours, and then I came upon a trail which had been considerably used at one time by both horses and cows. This gave me a renewed hope. I had not long to wait, for a little later from an eminence I saw a pool of dirty, stagnant water below me. It is not possible to express my feelings at that moment. I know I shouted "Water!" at the top of my lungs. Henry evidently felt the same way, for, tired as he was, he went forward at a full gallop. When I reached the pool, I saw that there were better-looking pools above, but I could control neither myself nor my horse any longer, and we fought face to head for the first drink.

A little later I found running water; satisfied, I hurried back to tell my partner the good news. We found it impossible to move Dutch, but Roy, the white horse Henry, and I went back to the water. It was good to see Roy and the white horse drink. We followed the brook up a little way, and discovered a group of buildings, long deserted, close to a copious ice-cold spring. It was lucky for Dutch that there chanced to be a five-gallon can in the cabin; we filled it and, carrying it between us, went back toward Dutch. I leave to your imagination the difficulties we experienced in carrying forty pounds of water on horseback across rough, broken, timbered country. Dutch was most pitiful in her eagerness for the water, which we gave to her virtually swallow by swallow, and she was a very different horse when she had had the full five gallons. It was now late, and so we were forced to camp at La Jara once more.

By afternoon of the next day we had taken possession of the cabin at the spring, and our horses were hobbled in luxuriant grass near-by. To permit Dutch to convalesce, we remained three days at Bear Springs (so we called it from the animals of that species which came there nightly to water). During that period, we made a reconnaissance of the region, and in so doing discovered an old Forest Service trail which would take us toward Jemez Springs. Roy's

cravings to get off the beaten path were satiated
this time; during our sojourn at Bear Springs
not a person came near us, and from all indica-
tions no one had been there for a long time. There
were some newspapers in the house; the most recent date on them was July 12, 1912.

Our departure was hastened by the fact that
our food-supply was becoming dangerously low,
and virtually all the food we had left was the
remains of a big mess of beans that we had cooked
three days before, and which were at the end of
the second day slightly spoiled. Roy affected to
eat them with relish; I frankly preferred to go
hungry.

We had one thing for which to thank Lee
Leyva: Señor Lee had a daughter whose resemblance to our white animal in form, pul-
chritude, and disposition was striking. The
daughter's name and thenceforth that of our
white horse was Lily—pronounced, not Lillie,
but Lee-Lee.

XII

THE ride over the dizzy trails from Bear Springs to Jemez pueblo would have been as pleasant as it was scenic, had not Lee-Lee developed the amusing habit of nipping Henry in the tail. It was somewhat disturbing to me to have Henry let fly both his heels at the offending Lee-Lee, and Lee-Lee would usually choose to be playful while we were traveling along the sheer edge of nothing. The first time that I felt my whole weight resting on Henry's front members, I had a decided inclination to dismount, but the desire completely disappeared when I noticed that to land on solid ground it would be necessary to descend about two thousand feet to the floor of the cañon below.

The isolated pueblo of Jemez did not seem especially picturesque or interesting as pueblos go, and we found our principal attraction in replenishing our pack-sacks at a trading-store presided over by a corpulent Indian. All that we had left in the way of provisions was pepper and baking-powder, which, while very excellent in their proper places, were hardly fitted to silence appetites such as ours.

That night we slept in a corral where our horses were munching alfalfa. In our usual fireside powwow Roy avowed his intention of writing a treatise on "Places I Have Slept In." We enumerated them: adobe huts of our Mexican friends, the residences of pueblo Indians, the brush shelters of shepherds of both of the aforementioned races, cabins of cattlemen, the haybarn of Lee Leyva, the porch of the cabin at Bear Springs, now the corral of the trader, and lastly, but mostly, the ground. Later the list was to become yet more fearful and wonderful.

The next morning it became apparent that Dutch was still in bad shape. Roy felt that it would be cruel to continue to ride her, and so when we arrived at Jemez Springs he began to try to arrange a trade. We were presented to a professional horse-trader, Bob Shreeves, who said that if we could wait until morning he would ride up into the mountain ranges with us. There he had a number of horses running, and he thought we could probably agree on an exchange.

The towering cliffs which overshadow Jemez Springs have seen much of history. Long before the white man came, an important Indian village flourished under their walls, and the older Pueblo Indians will tell you of a warrior queen of wondrous beauty who ruled the ancient pueblo; the Indian village, Jemez, destroyed in the Pueblo Rebellion of 1680, was succeeded by the Mexican settlement, Jemez; there an important chapter of the Penitente Order had its seat. Who but the red cliffs knows what rites these fanatics practised? The Mexican settlement remains, but the numberless hot springs have now made Jemez Springs a fashionable health resort. There are several modern hotels, one of which cannot be equaled in the Southwest save by the incomparable Harvey Houses.

As one may guess from its history there are many attractions for the traveler in Jemez Springs. The ruins of the mission church, built in 1618, fascinated us. But, as always happened when we became absorbed in reveries of the past, we found some concrete reminder of the fact that

we are living in an age of tourists rather than an
age of romance. In this case an orange-peel and
a kodak film box were the offending articles.
I venture to say that Howard Carter must have
found a chewing-gum wrapper, a film-box, or
some other token of the tourist in the innermost
chamber of the tomb of Tut-ankh-Amen. Time
after time, Roy and I would wrongly congratu-
late ourselves that we had at last arrived at a
place of interest that had not been descended
upon by crowds of tourists, but it never actually
came to pass until we found our way to remote
places of the Navajo Reservation.

We had an excellent guide the next morning
in the person of the estimable Mr. Shreeves. At
each place of interest we stopped while he told
us its history.

Out of the Soda Dam issue forty-seven cold
springs, twelve hot soda springs, and fifty-six
hot sulphur springs. Yes, the water is very bene-
ficial. Under that peak the monks of the Jemez
Mission buried their treasure before the Pueblo
Rebellion. Mr. Shreeves had not found time to go
after it yet, but he expected to get it within a
year. In the singing brook at our left he had

caught twenty-four brook-trout in one hour. At
this spot he had captured Mexican Pete. Mr.
Shreeves explained that, in addition to being a
horse-trader, he was also sheriff of the precinct
and a deputy game-warden.

We progressed ever upward through forests of
indescribable beauty. When we arrived at a spot
which was known as La Cueva, Mr. Shreeves
proposed that we stop and make camp while he
hunted for a certain buckskin horse. We had
supper almost ready when he returned with the
sorry-looking little horse which he proposed to
trade. Roy immediately assured Mr. Shreeves
that he would not insult the faithful Dutch by
considering such a proposition. Then Buck was
offered to us for fifteen dollars cash. We made it
apparent that we were not interested; in consequence the price was dropped to nine dollars.
We both felt that almost any kind of horse should
be worth nine dollars, but to show our sophistica-
tion we gave the animal what we considered a
very severe examination. Satisfied as to physical
defects, we tried him out. Despite his frail appearance, he nevertheless seemed able to walk,
trot, and gallop, although, as Roy expressed it,

you felt as if you were riding a jellyfish. The up-
shot of it all was that Buck became a member of
our family.

Long, long will I remember the misery of that
night at La Cueva. I wish that all the many who
have the impression that it never rains in New
Mexico could have been with us. Early in the
evening the temperature descended to a level
that is more common in March than in August;
from eight until nine there were intermittent
showers of hail; under our tarpaulins, combined
as a tent, we took refuge, and from the hail we
had satisfactory protection. But the steady down-
pour which succeeded the hail soon penetrated
the canvas. We were no longer able to keep up
even the semblance of a fire; we simply stood
under the trees and shivered throughout the long
night.

What a boon was the sunshine of the following
day! Our friend, Mr. Shreeves, bade us farewell
early in the morning, but we remained at La
Cueva until noon to bask in the sunlight while our
equipment dried out. We intended to relieve
Dutch by riding our new purchase, but we discovered what we should have noted the night

before if we had gone to the trouble of taking the saddle off: Buck had a hopelessly sore back. On that account we were exactly where we had been before, except that we now had another horse to lead, to care for, and to supply with food. Of course, in the mountains the feeding did not amount to a great deal, for the grass was so excellent that we almost dispensed with our usual ration of grain.

Roy and I have always numbered our days in the Jemez Mountains as among the most pleasant of our trip. It occurred to us that an explanation for the semi-aridity and barrenness of much of New Mexico would be that the Jemez Range robs all the rest of the State of due moisture that it may reach its perfection of beauty.

We idled our way along; on some days we did not travel ten miles. It was such a joy to fish for the elusive trout, or, better still, to swim with them. And then how good it was to walk through glorious meadows of flowers and drink deep of the refreshing fragrance of the pines! Never have I been able to dream such dreams as I did when lying under the silvery aspen looking down into abysmal, mystic cañons of varied shades of green.

We met few of our kind, but there was wild life in abundance. Birds without number sang to us, rodents of every description chattered at us, and at night the coyotes barked for us. And how weird it was to be awakened in the darkness by a cry that sounded for all the world like the shriek of a woman in distress! Haunting, terrifying, this cry of the mountain lion! We had plenty of opportunity to shoot wild turkey, bear, deer, mountain lion, and wildcat, but we had given up the desire to kill to the spirit of the forest.

Moist weather marred our last two days in the mountains. We discovered, however, a rain-stopping formula: (1) when it begins to rain behave unconcernedly and blithesomely; (2) allow yourself to get completely soaked; (3) go to the trouble of getting out your slicker and putting it on; (4) the rain will cease immediately.

At the crest of the divide we beheld a magnificent panorama of the country through which we were to travel. It was the desert we grew to love so well, the strange and desolate, the mysterious and colorful desert with its scorching heat and bitter cold. Its loneliness, its siren beauty, haunt me now.

XIII

FROM the top of the mountain the distant town of Cuba had been plainly visible, but on the plain below it was difficult to find. We had encircled it completely before we encountered a Mexican sheep-herder who was able to direct us to the metropolis.

We decided that Cuba was an excellent town when we discovered that it possessed a really good restaurant. It was a fine opportunity for Roy, because he had been at the mercy of my cooking ever since we left Santa Fé. Our system was that I cooked, while he washed and dried the dishes and tended the fire. That is, in cow-puncher idiom, he was bull-cook. He hated to cook, and I detested dish-washing; in consequence the arrangement was mutually satisfactory, but I often felt sorry for him when I had forgotten to put baking-powder in the biscuits or had burned the corn. As to choice of food, it was fortunate that our tastes were much alike, although, of course, variety is always somewhat limited in camp. Our principal articles of diet were biscuits, pancakes, bacon, tomatoes, corn, jams, and various canned meats. At times meals were graced with fresh meat or game or with eggs, fruit, or other ranch produce. When we did differ we compromised. Thus we had coffee in the morning and tea at night.

In the morning we bade the restaurant a reverent, regretful farewell. That night a distressing thing happened. In order to reach a water-hole we had found it necessary to travel until after dark. After pitching camp, Roy hurriedly wiped out the cooking-dishes while I was hobbling the horses. Supper over, he decided to wash the dishes, inasmuch as they had not been cleaned for several days, and he inquired of me as to the whereabouts of the dish-cloth; I directed him to the rag with which he had wiped out the dishes before supper. Finding it, he casually held it up in the fire-light. It disclosed itself as the rag we had been using for some weeks to clean Dutch's sore eye.

For three days the scenery was unchanging. A typical New Mexican landscape: gray plains, flanked by rolling hills, covered with sparse timber, or by mesas of manifold shape and color. The days were interesting yet not replete with incidents. We crossed the Jicarilla Apache Reservation, but we saw no Apaches. Two or three times a day we came to cattle-ranches. Invariably we were cordially welcomed and hospitably urged to remain for a meal or for the night. We often accepted the invitations; I recall especially a pleasant evening we spent as the guests of the Menefees, father and son. It had been a day of rain, of sinking sands, of roads of yellow water, of dripping sage, of roaring arroyos; and grateful indeed was the welcome of the Menefees: "Better get down and come in! Put your stuff in this shed, turn your horses loose, and get ready for supper."

Perhaps the feature of ranch life which thrilled us most was the singing—at chores in the morning, during the day's riding, around the fire at night. He has not lived who has not heard a cowboy chorus sing "Hi Yipppi Yi Yi Little Dogee" or "I Once Knew a Maiden" or "Little Joe the

Wrangler." The greatest favorite of all is the most mournful:

"Oh, bury me not on the lone prairee
Where the rattlesnakes hiss and the wind blows free."
These words came low and mournfully
From the pallid lips of a youth who lay
On his dying bed at the close of day.
"Oh, bury me not on the lone prairee
Where the wild coyotes can howl o'er me.
In a narrow grave, just six by three,
Oh, bury me not on the lone prairee."

During our progress through the cattle country we received much advice from old-timers. In particular we were told the best way of tying a pack. At first we absorbed all the information greedily, but soon the magic in the words "diamond hitch," "half-diamond hitch," and "squaw hitch" wore out. The principal cause of our disillusion was the discovery that the authorities were not in perfect agreement. One morning we left a ranch with the assurance that our pack was tied with a perfect squaw hitch. At noon we met an old cow-puncher who said, "Say, youngsters, let me tie a real squaw hitch for you." He completely retied our pack; that night at another ranch our host informed us that in the morning he would replace our amateurish arrangement with a "real squaw hitch." After that we used a hybrid arrangement of our own invention.

The fourth day after coming down from the mountains, we stopped at a ranch to get directions for the remainder of our journey to Farmington. The rancher said that the usual way was to travel up Cañon Largo, but there was a shorter route. "You can't miss it," he said. Wherefore for five days we were confined within cañon walls. Cañon Largo is almost one hundred miles long and in places several miles wide. Homesteads dot its alkali reaches. Their inhabitants are evidently not prosperous; they call themselves "misery seekers."

Heavy rains made the going in Cañon Largo somewhat difficult, for trails were virtually obliterated, and there was quicksand in the wide arroyo (wash) in the middle of the cañon which had to be crossed and recrossed. Quicksand is both terrifying and fascinating. Imagine a smooth stretch of apparently good hard sand upon which your horse had so far made little impression—then to suddenly feel his fore feet sink above his hoofs; a terrified snort, and then suddenly his rear end sinks a foot. You jump off quickly to lighten his load, and find yourself mired to your knees, while your horse alternately rises and sinks in the sand, producing hoarse whistlings. Luckily you obtain a foothold on a trustworthy spot, haul his head around, and by dint of shrieks, blows, and tugging manage to get him to flounder after you to solid earth.

On one occasion we had a near catastrophe. In order to facilitate leading Buck, I had tied his lead-rope to my saddle. When we were exactly half-way across the arroyo, Buck became bogged and jerked back with such force that the latigo strap on my McClellan was broken, and off came saddle and I. Relieved of his burden, Henry with much snorting and kicking ran to the opposite bank and left to Roy, Dutch, and Lee-Lee the task of dragging me from the quicksand. This rescue work they performed most nobly, although I had gone in up to my knees. Buck plunged off, pulling after him the saddle and the various articles that were strapped to it. We said good-by to nine dollars, but to our surprise we found that Buck had gained the opposite bank and was calmly standing by Henry. We concluded that he had been going too fast to be stopped by anything. For the rest of the day I rode in a saddle that was extremely muddy, but as I was extremely muddy too it did not matter much. My camera peeled off with it. Indeed I firmly believe that my camera was cursed by the gods of Acoma, Taos, and Santo Domingo, whose mysteries it had violated, for any accident on the trip always included the camera.

There were other lively incidents: I tried to pull Dutch up a steep embankment, but she fell backward, pulling me with her. We were equally uninjured, but the lard and syrup-pails in the pack-sacks were forced open, and all our food was liberally coated with their contents. Roy rode Henry one day and had several disputes with him upon matters of policy. I well remember one of Roy's coaxing soliloquies:

"Come on, Henry; you can go straight up here perfectly well. Come on, now! So you won't go up, eh, Henry?" Wham! *Wham!* WHAM! This with a persuader.

At another time we cursed the rain even more fervently. We had met a rancher who invited us to come to his home and spend the night with him. But when we arrived at a branch of the main arroyo which lay between us and our friend's house, we found the water so high that it was impossible to cross. We had to make camp on the damp ground and eat a camp supper, while a hundred yards away were a warm comfortable house and the ingredients for an excellent meal.

While in Cañon Largo we evolved an invention which was of the utmost value to us. For some time the problem of controlling Henry's peregrinating propensities had worried us. At first we had staked him at the end of a sixty-foot rope; unfortunately he did not thrive on this treatment; he would become entangled in the rope and disturb our slumbers by stamping and snorting. On the other hand, the plan of hobbling him, as we did the other horses, had two distinct disadvantages. In the first place, he always led the other horses as far from camp as possible. In the second, it took much time and even more nervous energy to catch him. When Roy approached him, he would jump a few feet, stop, look back, and snort. This process would be repeated several times until Roy would get disgusted and run after him. Unhappily Henry could jump faster than Roy could run. Unless he happened to be in a peculiarly decent mood, it was usually necessary for us to get on the other horses and run him down. When I was preparing breakfast it used to amuse me to hear Roy yelling something after this fashion: "Whoa, Henry! Whoa, Henry! Nice boy! Whoa, Henry! *Whoa, Henry!* WHOA, YOU—" It ceased to amuse, however, after one morning when I was the victim of his idiosyncrasies. His disposition was particularly bad that morning, and in chasing him down a hill I stumbled and fell on the rocks. We then together swore a mighty oath that Henry should no more roam. And so it was that we evolved the side-line. This was a rope arrangement which secured one of his hobbled front feet to one of his rear feet. It was a task to put it on, as Henry was rather touchy about his rear limbs, but it worked to perfection. It gave us great joy that first morning to chase Henry and to watch him stumble and fall.

We were glad to arrive at the town of Blanco at the mouth of Cañon Largo. The cañon widened; the yellow ribbon of water splashed its muddy

hue upon some straggling cottonwoods; an adobe
Mexican home clung to our path; we circled
through the corral and down the hill; we crossed
a wooden bridge and pulled up thankfully in
front of a log trading-post for a drink of brack-
ish well-water. We entered the store, which was
tended by a patriarch whose nicotine-colored
whiskers hid behind his vest. The only other oc-
cupant was a stout, good-natured city salesman,
with whom we entered into casual conversation.
When we left, he followed us out. As Roy was
swinging into the saddle he happened to notice
that the salesman's car bore a Colorado license.
Now, Roy's boyhood home had been in Silverton, Colorado, and he was perpetually in hope of
finding some one from there. And so now he
said:

"Don't happen to come from Silverton, old
man?"

"Yep, that's my home and has been for thirty
years."

"Well, I'll be damned! You don't happen to
know Bob Murray or Slim Clauson or Gene
Grimes or—"

"Gene Grimes is *my* name.   Who the hell are

you anyway? Andy Anderson! Well, where in
the name of sin have you been keeping yourself
these twenty years? You was only ten when you
left Silverton, wasn't you?"

And this was the beginning of reminiscences
lasting all afternoon.

The next day we reached the delightful little
town of Aztec. It was the first truly American
town we had been in on our trip, and we enjoyed
seeing again well kept American homes and tidy
friendly American people. The ruin of an ancient pueblo near Aztec is very interesting, and
even more interesting is the collection of pottery,
mummies, and handiwork which has been taken
from the ruin.

We followed down the beautiful valley of the
Animas River toward Farmington; beautiful it
was, but always when we found a beautiful river
valley we also found swarms of mosquitoes. At
night we put up our tent as a protection against
them, but, accustomed as we were to sleeping in
the open, the atmosphere of the tent seemed hot
and stifling.

When we arrived in Farmington, we made a
dash for the post-office; neither of us had heard

from home or friends for more than a month. We spent several hours devouring our mail, and then decided to remain there for two or three days, for our horses needed a rest on good pasture, and we could well use some time in writing letters and making inquiries about the country we expected to go through; our plans for the future were altogether indefinite.

Farmington is a town of perhaps seven hundred people, a trading-center for a considerable area, and the market-place for the great amount of fruit raised by the surrounding ranches. In the summer, fruit may be had in Farmington for almost nothing. We were offered choice peaches, pears, plums, and melons for a cent a pound. At the time of our visit, the town was in the throes of an oil boom, and every citizen was counting on future wealth. We spent a great deal of our time loafing on the streets, talking with every one we could, for we were trying to accumulate every possible bit of information about the Navajo country. During this process we became acquainted with a young gentleman who made us an interesting proposition, although it was a little startling to young Americans of our respectability. We could not, however, blame any one for thinking we might be of the underworld, for we were travel-worn and ragged. But be that as it may, we were given a cordial invitation to participate in the robbing of a pool-hall in Telluride, Colorado. Our friend knew the lay of the land, and knew that on a certain date when the miners were paid off there would be enough money in the till to make it worth while. Roy entered into the spirit of the thing well enough.

"How much do you think we might get, Jack? We have some other plans that are pretty profitable, and we hadn't really planned to go to Colorado."

"Damn close to a thousand dollars, or I miss my guess. But look here, I don't want you fellows to come along if you're goin' to get chicken-livered. I talked to you because you looked like you had some guts, and fellows don't wander round the country like you guys without getting some practice."

"Well, now," said Roy, "don't worry about that part of it. In fact, I might as well tell you, since you trusted us, that I'm wanted in New York right now. And as for my partner here, he's one of the smoothest gentleman-crooks in New York State. The only reason we're out here is that that country won't be healthy for us for a while."

"All right then. What do you say? If you're comin' you'll have to start to-morrow or next day. But we'll have to go separately. If they saw me bringin' a couple strange guys into town, somebody might get suspicious."

"Well, partner, what do you say?" quoth Roy.

"O.K. with me."

"Shake then. We'll meet you in Telluride the fourteenth."

(Two months later, in an old paper which we picked up in an Indian trading-post, we read that the job had been completed without our assistance, and that it had netted seven hundred dollars. Then we rather regretted our virtue.)

About the Navajo Reservation we heard many strange stories and received much conflicting advice, but it was not until we went to interview Nat Bridgeman, who had been a trader on the reservation for ten years, that we learned anything which was definite enough to help us.

"Mr. Bridgeman, we plan to go across the

Navajo Reservation. Do you think we can make it all right, and where would you advise us to go?"

"How long you been travelin' horseback, boys, and does you speak any Navajo? Answer me them, and I can tell you."

"We've been packing for several months now, and one of us knows enough Navajo to ask where water and grass is and things like that."

"Well, then I reckon you'd make out all right. There's generally a plenty of water there now, and, if you pick up Navvie as fast as you can, you shouldn't have much trouble."

"What about the Rainbow Bridge?"

"Well, now, that's a horse of another color. That'd all depend upon whether you could get Wetherill or one of the boys that works for him to take you."

"Have you ever been there?"

"No, but I'm sure a-goin' before I die. You know twenty years ago the Navvies used to be tellin' me about this dog-gone arch of stone with every color of the rainbow in it, but I didn't pay no attention; I thought it was just some cock-and-bull legend of theirn. But Mrs. Wetherill up at Kayenta, she believed 'em, and made Wetherill go look, and after about dyin' back in the God-forsaken country, damned if he didn't find it. I guess it's the greatest sight on earth, boys."

"We'll be starting to-morrow. What is the quickest way to get to Kayenta?"

"Well, go from here down the river to Shiprock, and there they'll direct you west. But say, boys, have you been up to Colorado in the Mesa Verde country?"

"Why, no, we haven't."

"Now, you ought to go up there first. The Navvies and the Bridge'll keep, and it is a mighty shame if you came as close as this to that Green Mesa country and didn't see it. It ain't more than a hundred and twenty miles from here, just a little across the Colorado line."

XIV

W E traveled the sixty miles from Farmington to the Colorado line without encountering anything unusual either in scenery or in adventure. Soon after entering Colorado we came into a region which was entirely different from any we had heretofore visited. In the first place, we saw more dwellings and more people in a single day than we had been accustomed to seeing in several weeks; in the second, the general aspect of the landscape was unlike any New Mexico scenery with which we were familiar. Lovely green valleys, surrounded by the snow-capped peaks of the La Plata Mountains, were divided up into prosperous farms. At the time of our arrival, the farmers were cutting alfalfa, which they sold to us for almost nothing; it was fortunate for us that they did so, because instead of having the limitless, unfenced pasture of the trail for our horses we now had only the scanty grass between the fences that lined the road.

The farmers were all friendly and courteous, but hardly as hospitable as our cow-puncher friends. They were all very curious about the reason for our mode of traveling. When, in answer to their questions, we gave the truthful reply that we were riding for our health, they either laughed or showed disbelief by the expression of their faces. One fellow said: "Why yarn about it, boys? I won't give you away if you are prospecting or bootlegging." We had forgotten that our appearance belied any suggestion of ill health. Roy had lost twenty-five pounds in weight, mostly around the waist-line, while I had gained thirty pounds. We were hardened and tanned by outdoor life, so that we little resembled the pale soft things that had come from the East.

Buck's back had been giving us considerable worry. We treated it with every kind of salve we could procure, but the sore would not heal. One day Dutch was indisposed and we had to ride Buck. At the close of the day we were gratified to find that the sore, instead of becoming worse as we had feared, had healed over. Thereafter we

rode Buck quite frequently. He proved a trustworthy steed, although, when riding him, one felt
as stable as if supported by four pieces of cooked
macaroni.

A week after leaving Farmington we arrived
in Mancos, Colorado. Mancos was a treat to us.
Roy was able to get good cigars again, and I to
indulge in a weakness for chocolate ice-cream.
The town is a sleepy but pretty place; its streets
reminded me strongly of those in my Iowa home.

The first night out of Mancos on our way to
Mesa Verde National Park we were supper hosts
to a Ute Indian. He was a pleasant fellow for
an educated Indian, and we invited him to camp
with us. After breakfast the next morning he
told us that he was hurrying back to the Ute
Reservation in order to be present at the annual
Sun Dance. He offered to conduct us to the
scene of the dance if we cared to go, and we
eagerly seized the opportunity.

That evening we were camped on the level
plain of Tewaoc in the shadow of the Green
Mesa; a mile away flickered the camp-fires of the
Utes, who were gathered for their annual hom-
age to the great Sun God. Our Ute friend ad-

vised us not to approach the immediate neighborhood of the dance until the ceremonies were well under way, but when we heard the shrill pipe of the flute, the roar of the tom-toms, the harsh crashing of the cymbals, we could wait no longer. Those fires lured us; the tom-toms called.

Just as the moon was rising, we began our tramp across the sage-brush flat. It was cool and misty; the night air was redolent with the tang of the sage. On our left towered Mesa Verde, two thousand feet above the plain; on the other side loomed Ute Peak, black and mysterious. The rising moon drew aside the veil of shadow and revealed that which must be more than a rock—the Shiprock of the Desert. All of these became more glorious in the unthinkable splendor of the full Colorado moon. It was intoxicating. What a setting for a barbaric pageant!

Soon we were among the smoldering campfires of the Indians, but the tepees and wagons were quite deserted. As the music became louder, we grew rather timid, but we could not turn back; we slunk along. At last we came to a high circular fence of pine-boughs, forming an inclosure perhaps a hundred yards in diameter. At the left

of the center of the inclosure was a roaring log
fire which nearly blinded us at first. We were
afraid to enter, but the hundred or more Utes
crouched around the fire seemed to be entirely
oblivious of our presence. And so we wrapped
ourselves more closely in our blankets, entered
the inclosure, and seated ourselves out of the
light under the cover of the brush fence.

In the exact center of the circle was a tall,
peculiarly forked pine pole painted in four colors
to represent the four seasons of the sun. Then out
of the darkness toward this pole came twelve
nude male dancers with their eyes riveted upon
the paintings. Back and forth they went in varied
order and movements, but never did they remove
their eyes from the pole. For hours we scarcely
stirred, fascinated by the beauty of the dance,
the graceful wavings of the prayer-plumes, the
songs of the stamping, chanting chorus of thirty
men and women who were invisible in the darkness to the rear of the inclosure. The shrill whistles, the beats of the tom-toms, were patently sav-
age, but how they thrilled us! I can hear them
still.

The seemingly stolid spectators were an interesting study. They sat motionless, totally absorbed in the spectacle. The braided jet hair of the men glistened in the firelight, and the jewels of the women sparkled. We wanted to ask them the meaning of the ceremonies, which were as unintelligible to us as they were beautiful, but were afraid to do so, because the few glances which some of them had given us had been none too friendly.

We were held all through the night, but just before dawn we left, that the harshness of daylight might not rob the dance of its mystic, incomprehensible beauty. At Tewaoc we learned that for three days and two nights the dancers continue, stopping neither for food nor drink, ever keeping their eyes on the sacred pole. Before the dance ends, some of the dancers drop from exhaustion. But they have expiated the sins of the Ute!

A day later we began the toilsome ascent of Mesa Verde. We had been attracted to the park by its antiquities, but we were repaid for the trip before we beheld any of them by the magnificent panorama from Point Lookout on top of the mesa. Colorado, Utah, Arizona, and New

Mexico combine to make a scene of such beauty and grandeur that one is silenced, stunned, awed. Two thousand feet below lie the fertile Montezuma and Mancos valleys, surrounded by the majestic Colorado mountains; more distant is a gray haze which is Utah, where the horizon is dominated by the Blue Mountains, 115 miles away; to the rear appears the Navajo Reservation in New Mexico and Arizona, mountain-inclosed sandy plain. How the colors, the greens, the blues, the grays, blend to form a soul-searching and soul-cleansing picture that is like unto a vision! One cannot look out into that sublime immensity without thinking a little and forgetting much.

XV

FROM Point Lookout we progressed south-
ward along the edge of the cañon-
seamed mesa until at nightfall we
reached the center of activity at Spruce Tree
Camp. On registering at park headquarters
the following day we were dismayed to find
that we should not be allowed to visit the
ruins unless accompanied by one of the park
guides. The ranger said that it was a mere for-
mality. "Just drive your car in the rear of that
group of cars out there and join the parties when
they stop." We explained that we were without
such a vehicle. The ranger was kind but firm;
we would have to induce a party of tourists to
let us ride with them. To our regret we were
hardly prepared to join the company of respectable people. Neither of us had received expected
pecuniary assistance in Farmington, and our
wardrobes were in a sad state. In particular, our

foot-gear worried us: Roy's big toe stuck out of his boot, and the sole of one of my shoes was entirely gone, so that my naked foot came in contact with the earth when I walked.

Perhaps we should never have seen the Mesa Verde ruins had not the kind-hearted proprietor of an overcrowded Ford offered to transport us. Members of the party stared at us, and decency demanded that we give them an explanation of our condition. Roy, ever voluble, told them an interesting tale about a wager. He told it so well that we were thereupon accepted socially by the group of middle-aged tourists who made up the party.

The ruins were indescribably fascinating; they were far grander than any we had seen. One overhanging cliff sheltered a communal house three hundred feet long and fifty to a hundred feet wide. It must have been a hardy and a clever race to make a living from the dry soil of the cañon floors and to construct such well built homes in seemingly inaccessible places. Especially interesting to us were the bins where they had stored their grain, the mills where they had ground their flour, and the roosts they had made for their domesticated wild turkeys. The balcony of the house delighted the women of the party. It made them shiver to look at the perpendicular drop to the floor of the cañon, and they enjoyed being shocked by the echo which returns "Go to hell" nine times when the guide shouts "Board of Health."

We were lounging in front of park headquarters when we were accosted by two of the guides with whom we had had a casual acquaintance.

"My name's Hugh Cummings."

"And mine is Doc Cornell. We've been intending to introduce ourselves and get acquainted ever since we heard you telling that ridiculous story about having wagered to wear your shoes until next month, even though there was nothing left but the tops. We've bummed ourselves, and we know what it all means, and we've been wondering if we couldn't give you a lift temporarily; at least let us loan you some extra shoes of ours, or your feet themselves will be gone by the time you leave these rocks."

"You seem to have the cold dope on us, fellows. We'll have some money as soon as we get back to our base of supplies, Farmington, and we have plenty now to live with, but we can't buy shoes."

"Have you been on the trail long? You look as if you might."

"More than six months for Andy, and about half that many for me."

"You certainly must have had some rare experiences."

"We have had some interesting times, but we are sure the best is yet to be."

"Where are you going from here?"

"Well, first back to Farmington, but then we are going to hit out across the Navajo desert, and eventually we hope that we can get to the Rainbow Bridge."

"Rainbow Bridge! Say, don't we wish we were going with you! You know Rainbow Bridge has been made a National Monument, and we were looking at some pictures of it and reading its history in some Park Service publications last week."

"Pictures of the Bridge?"

"Come on in. We'll show them to you now."

Roy expressed naturally, albeit crudely, our reaction to the pictures. He said simply, "My God!"

Later Roy and I agreed that it would be splendid if Cummings and Cornell could join us at the end of the park season and make the trip to the Bridge. We would hardly be ready to go before fall anyway, and they, by going to Flagstaff and coming up with the mail, could get to Kayenta in a reasonably short time. We broached the idea to them, and, to our delight, they ended by agreeing to meet us in Kayenta early in September.

That night some of our new friends insisted that we join them at the hotel, and we had a pleasant evening. Roy was the star performer—he instructed a class of maidens in the real Hawaiian *hula,* while scandalized mamas gasped.

Several more days we spent in visiting the numerous cliff-dwellings and pueblo ruins, as well as the spots of natural beauty in which the Mesa Verde abounds. I remember most vividly blue sky, bronze roads in dark green glades, distant black gulches, wondrous tiny villages clinging to shelves a thousand feet above the cañon below, the perfect masonry of mysterious Sun Temple, the superb vista of Cliff Palace from Sun Temple Point, unique Square Tower House, and lonely Navajo Watch Tower, which commands a view for fifty miles in every direction. On many of these rambles we had the good fortune to be in the company of a character who is really a part of Mesa Verde, Mr. A. B. Hardin. Mr. Hardin was one of the first white men to ascend the mesa, and he has played a large part in the discovery of the ruins and also in the popularizing of the park.

We left Buck on Mesa Verde, pensioned for life. His back had become sore again, and we felt that the best we could do for him would be to leave him in the park, which is a sanctuary for animals of all kinds. Poor Buck, we are sure that your twelve years were not happy ones, for there was always a look of piteous pleading in your eyes. There was always something very pathetic about your gameness and your evident desire to please. Let your epitaph be, "He done his damnedest."

In order to save time we returned to Farmington by the same way we had come. The return trip was uneventful; in Farmington we found money waiting for us, and we both invested in boots.

XVI

IT was on a Sunday morning in mid-September when we said good-by to Farmington and to civilization. By noon we had passed through the Mormon villages of Fruitland and Kirtland. We were not to enter another white settlement for months—unless one calls a Navajo trading-post with one white family a settlement.

The next day, midway between Farmington and the Shiprock trading-post and Indian agency, occurred the first accident to mar our trip. After breakfast, as Roy was screwing the top of our lard-jar, the vessel collapsed, and a piece of glass entered the palm of his hand. The bleeding was terrific; I put on a tourniquet, and it was necessary to keep it extremely tight. After a trip that was very painful to Roy, we arrived at Shiprock and immediately sought out the physician supposed to be in residence at the government Indian agency. He was out making a call, but the nurse dressed the wound and relieved the pain somewhat. That evening the doctor's examination revealed that a nerve in Roy's hand had been cut and that there were also possibilities of infection. He strongly advised against the carrying out of our planned itinerary, for if we did carry it out we would not come within range of a doctor for several weeks at least. We remained in Shiprock a day, but Roy could stand it no longer and insisted that we forge onward. And so we took the comparatively plain wagon-road, which the trader assured us would carry us almost due westward to the post of Redrock.

Just south of the Shiprock Indian Agency flows the San Juan River, the wide treacherous river of the desert flowing toward Utah to join the mighty Colorado in the purple cañons of the Rainbow Bridge region. We crossed it and were actually in the Navajo empire. And an empire it is—the last domain in these United States where Wilderness and Wildness yet reign supreme. Imagine, if you can, a semi-arid grazing area larger than the States of Massachusetts and Connecticut combined, whose total population consists of thirty-five thousand pastoral, nomadic Indians plus a handful of white men—traders and members of the Indian Service. It is a region unspoiled by civilization: no shrieking locomotives disturb its serene, peaceful freedom; it is far indeed from the madding crowd. In this paradise the only wholly self-supporting tribe of Indians in the Southwest live a happy and industrious life. They are extremely prosperous and are a valuable economic asset to the country. In 1923 it is estimated that they marketed products to the value of four million dollars. Sheep, wool, their justly famous blankets, and silver handiwork are their principal contributions to the outside world.

The bare red desert, south and west of the Shiprock Agency, spreads out impressively toward the deep-blue Lu-ka-chu-kai and Tunicha Mountains, which mark the line between New Mexico and Arizona. Sixteen hundred and four feet above this vast flat rises that great jagged shaft of rock, the Shiprock of the Desert, which we had seen from the place of the Ute Sun Dance and from the top of the Mesa Verde. Its resemblance to a sailing-vessel was perceptible from Colorado, but now, especially in the moon-light, the illusion of a wind-jammer under full sail was perfect. Another natural wonder near the Shiprock was what we called "the train of cars," a long line of element-molded sandstone rock which has a distinct resemblance to a loco-motive drawing a line of freight-cars.

We thought the Shiprock a fitting symbol of the impenetrable solitude of the region. Some bleached skulls by an evil-smelling water-hole made us feel that we were in the real desert, life-less and lonely. We had seen many Navajos in the immediate vicinity of the Shiprock Agency, but this region appeared to be completely de-serted by them. We were a little alarmed when we found our horses gone one morning, as it was a long walk back to civilization, but after almost a day of tracking and searching for them far from our camp, in the late afternoon Roy, re-turning to camp, stumbled upon them in a little depression not a quarter of a mile from where we had turned them loose. Lee-Lee had rid herself of her bell during the night.

Our progress was slow these days, for the elaborate and perfect systems we had devised for expediting our packing, unpacking, and camp-chores were now out of the question, since Andy was entirely deprived of the use of his right hand. For several mornings it was necessary for me to get the horses, cook, wash the dishes, pack the panniers, saddle the horses, hang the panniers on the sawbuck, throw on the bed, and tie the whole. All the while Roy fussed and fumed at his enforced inactivity. Even when his cut did heal, the fingers refused to bend, and so we gradually evolved new systems that were almost as efficient as those of old.

Four days after quitting Shiprock we arrived at Redrock, a typical Navajo trading-post. There was the usual picture—a long low building with hitching-posts in front, to which were tied gaunt-looking ponies. All around lounged Navajo men, women, and children, gossiping and chattering about the weather much after the manner of their white kindred. They were an attractive group. The Navajos are much more favored by nature than the Pueblo Indians or the Utes. Both the men and the women have lithe slender figures, and their features, as a rule, are regular. We found, however, a great diversity of facial

contour among the Navajos, due, doubtless, to
the infusion of the blood of neighboring tribes.
Many types are distinctly Chinese, and others
have a Filipino cast of feature. The attire of this
group, and particularly of the men in it, presented many contrasts. Many of the men wore
cheap store clothing, fur caps or sombreros; but
others wore the handsome graceful costume of
the elder generation—a silk handkerchief around
the head, a velvet blouse fastened with silver buttons, loose pantaloons of linen or velvet, moccasins. The dress of the women was more uniform.
They wore waists of calico or velvet, and flowing
skirts which covered a multitude of petticoats.
Men, women, and children were bedecked with
beautiful hammered silver jewelry—finger-rings
of varied shapes, bracelets of fantastic design,
belts composed of oval disks, necklaces made up
of hollow spherical beads placed between conven-
tionalized squash-blossoms. All of these were
often set with turquoise. Even more than by their
costumes we were attracted by their sunny dispo-
sitions. They put much of friendliness and good-
will into their "Iata Heys" of greeting.

We entered the store.

"Well, I'll be damned. White men on horse-back! Where you bound for? Kayenta? Heard of the Bridge, I'll bet. Well, I don't blame you; wish I were going along with you. How to go from here? Yes, I can tell how about that easy enough. You'll want to go over the mountains and then down to Chin Lee. It ain't a bad trail. I wouldn't hurry along though. The Bridge'll wait, and there's a lot of pretty country between here and Chin Lee, and when you get there you sure want to go up the cañons."

We now secured the services of the trader as interpreter, for the time had come for us to trade Dutch. She was developing a sore back, and we felt that it would be a kindness to her to exchange her for a fresh animal. After more than an hour of haranguing we traded Dutch, eight dollars, and a pair of Mesa Verde shoes for a pony, de-spite the fact that the government only values Navajo ponies at two and a half dollars each. Babe was an infant lady of sweet disposition; Andy said that he felt guilty of cradle-robbery. Our last sight of Mama Dutch was a fast loping figure disappearing over a sandy rise.

The trader gave us specific directions for

choosing our roads to reach the pass over the mountains, but we had not been gone from Redrock more than an hour before we decided that the only feasible system for us was to travel as nearly as possible in the general direction of the pass. We always found it thus on the reservation. There are perfect mazes of wagon-roads—not to mention the trails, which are literally without number—leading to Navajo homes, to wood, and to water, as well as to the trading-stores which are usually our immediate objectives. The great trouble is that there is no possible means of distinguishing between them. Plainness is not a safe guide; the plainest road often took us to a Navajo residence and left us there. Automobile tracks are a good sign of the trail of the white man, but unfortunately few automobiles penetrate this portion of the Navajo country in a year.

The Indians were always ready to help us find our way, but language was an obstacle. A few of the older traveled Navajos speak Mexican, and a few of the younger ones speak English, but of these many will not. I knew some hundred and fifty words of their language, and between that and the medium of signs we sometimes got useful information, for a Navajo can often tell you more with his hands than a white man can with his tongue.

Roy and I decided that we must learn their language. First I taught him the little that I knew. We have often laughed over his attempt to put into practice the first lesson. We met a group of Navajos on horseback; I responded to their greeting with the conventional "Iata Hey." Andy, wishing to be different, said "Najonii!" (Pretty). I explained to him that the word had about the same significance as "pussycat" would have had if we had been greeting American travelers under like circumstances.

At the end of a few days Roy could distinguish between and pronounce tolerably well a number of expressions. He knew that *iata hey* meant almost anything: "how do you do," "all right," "good-by." He knew that *najonii* meant "pretty" or "nice." In addition he knew that *shi* meant "I" or "mine" and that *ni* meant "you" or "yours," that *hogan* meant "house," that *cleen* meant "horse," and that *au* meant "yes." Roy was delighted to find that he could now carry on a conversation in the language of the aborigine. A stenographic report of a sample discourse is as follows:

Roy: "Iata hey!" How are you!

Sir Navajo: "Iata hey!" Fine; how's yourself?

Roy: "Iata hey!" Good!

Sir Navajo: "Iata hey!" Well, that's good.

Roy: "Ni cleen?" Your horse? (probably, or at least we hope so).

Sir Navajo: "Au." Yes (very graciously, considering the possible implication).

Roy: "Shi cleen." My horse!

Sir Navajo: "Iata hey." Good-by.

Roy: "Iata hey!" Same to you, old thing!

We enjoyed the contact with the Navajos we met on the road. The men were very curious but just as friendly and courteous, while the women and children were shy and prone to giggling. Most of them were on horseback, and they all rode with an enviable seat, but now and then we met a rickety old wagon drawn by two tiny ponies carrying its full load toward a trading-store or the *hogan* of a friend. Besides fellow-travelers we often met shepherds, usually children, with their

flocks of sheep and goats. Sometimes we saw
Navajo *hogans* or houses. A Navajo *hogan*
greatly reminds you of a croquette with the top
cut off or of a brown Eskimo igloo. We were
more eager to become better acquainted with
these, but we hesitated to trespass on the apparent friendliness of the owners. From the outside these conical earth-covered lodges built on
a framework of cedar logs appeared a stable and
inviting protection from the elements.

It was on a night when we were in the foot-
hills of the Lu-ka-chu-kai Mountains that Andy
first saw the inside of a Navajo residence. A bitter cold wind was making us shiver when we
caught sight of an apparently deserted *hogan*.
We cautiously approached; no one appeared; we
peeped within. A clean dirt floor; it looked cozy
and tempting; it was empty. As the sun was
sinking, we took possession. How warm and
comfortable it was when we had a small fire under the hole in the apex of the dwelling! As our
bacon and potatoes were browning we heard the
rumble of wheels in the chuck-holes, the bleat of
lambs, and the bark of a dog. The rug which
served as the door of the *hogan* was lifted, and a

Navajo man entered. In the firelight we could not see which emotion he was registering.

"Ni hogan?" (Your house?), I mumbled.

"Au!" (Yes!)

It could be no worse. I dimly wondered exactly what I should do, if, on returning to my home at the close of a hard day, I found strangers sitting on my floor, and strangers' effects taking up all of the four hundred square feet of my dwelling.

"Iata hey," said our host. He extended his hand. We took it rather suspiciously, Roy especially. He was not too sure of my understanding of the Navajo language in general and of the elastic gamut of the term *iata hey* in particular.

Our friend (we hoped) lifted the rug and spoke rapidly to some one without. Entered mama and five offspring. Mr. Indian now addressed a few remarks to us, but we assured him by signs that we did not understand. We then queried him—"Speak English? Habla Español?" Much shaking of the head convinced us that he did not possess either accomplishment. Our position was somewhat doubtful. How we longed for a "Book of Etiquette" in two volumes to solve our problem! But—criminal carelessness!—we did not have this authority at hand. We therefore decided, after a hurried consultation, that the proper course of conduct for us would be not to embarrass our hosts by appearing ill at ease. We continued, or rather enlarged upon, our preparations for supper. Would our host and family honor us by partaking of our repast? Yes, but they served the children first and refused second helpings until we had eaten.

Dishes washed, we showed our good breeding by attempting to keep up a conversation. Of course, we were not at all verbose. When the correct hour arrived, we indicated we should withdraw to the open air for our slumbers. Our friends, however, would not have it so. We therefore slept between papa and mama with the children curled up at our feet.

In the morning madam served us a breakfast that was indeed excellent. The first course was goat's milk, fresh from the herd without; the second course was more elaborate—roasted goat meat *à la Navajo* (meaning half raw), coffee, and squaw bread, a fried concoction which tastes like waffles but better.

XVII

O N the day after our *hogan* adventure we entered the wonderland of Arizona. We did not know exactly when or where, as the sign-posts of our best regulated highways were entirely lacking. The trader at Redrock had told us that when we crossed the divide in the mountains we should no longer be in New Mexico; therefore, assuming that we had not crossed the wrong mountains, we were in Arizona. We could not have guessed it from the character of the country; if dropped on the high plateau which is the top of the Lu-ka-chu-kai Mountains, one would be more likely to suppose himself in Maine or northern Michigan than in "desert" Arizona. It is a region of clear blue lakes surrounded by splendid forests. The first lake we came upon tempted us first to a swim and then to exploration of the surrounding country. We discovered another body of water, yet more

beautiful, and then another. Thus were we led
far from our planned route, which was to take us
to Chin Lee, where we hoped to find a doctor to
examine Roy's hand. Those days in the mountains!—towering pines, chilly winds, squirrels
and eagles, rushing brooks, river reeds, passes
guarded by grotesque formations, sweet-william,
paint-brush, columbine, pine-cones, and blue
cedar balls.

At last we were content to descend to the west-
ward-stretching plains. When we did, the landscape we beheld was sufficiently Arizonian—
against the base of the mountains, rugged, vividly
colored sandstone heights wind-shaped into suggestive, fanciful outlines; beyond lay the inevit-
able gray sage desert of distance.

We found our way to the Lu-ka-chu-kai trading-post, presided over by Mr. Cassidy. A typical
Navajo trading-post: an adobe building with one
long room full of merchandise; the living-quar-
ters are in the rear, corral adjoining; shelves are
stacked high with canned goods of every description—candies, flour, salt, sugar, coffee, tobacco,
saddles, bridles, buckets, bolts of velvet and ging-
ham, buttons, thread; the usual quantity of

jewelry pawned by the Navajos awaits redemption. The value of this pawned jewelry in many of the trading-stores, especially during the "starvation moon" of February, is truly enormous. We had not spoken English except to each other for more than a week, and it was good to speak it again.

Later in the day we came to another trading-post, Greasewood Springs. We did not fully realize at this time what a rare occurrence this was, to ride to two trading-posts in a single day. At both places we obtained considerable help in the study of the Navajo language, which we were now making systematic efforts to learn. We kept a note-book in which we jotted down new words and phrases. At night around the camp-fire we would quiz each other on the new vocabulary which the day had brought. It was great fun to practise on the Navajos; at least it was fun for us, and I rather believe they enjoyed it too.

We left Greasewood late in the afternoon, after obtaining our general directions for Chin Lee and information regarding sources of water-supply. We had not been on our way long when we were joined by a Navajo. He wore a fur cap, green turquoise earrings, a yellow kerchief, a red string that bound his hair into a knob, blue skirt, yellow trousers, puttees, and shoes.

"Ha-gosh-a?" (Where are you going?) he queried.

"Chin Lee go!" (Going to where the water comes out), we replied, proud of our understanding.

"Shi Chin Lee go" (I also am going to the place where the water comes out), he affirmed.

All of which meant that we should have a guide for our journey to Chin Lee, provided that we did not misunderstand him, and provided that we could contrive to keep him with us. The first of these provisos did not bother us that afternoon, since it took all our energies to keep John, as we dubbed him, in our party. He soon made it apparent that, having gone through with the usual civilities of conversation, he would fain leave us and hurry on to his destination. Our rate of travel was calculated to keep us and our horses comfortable rather than to get us anywhere. We pressed candy and tobacco upon John, and after each gift he seemed to feel that

politeness demanded that he tarry a few more
moments. But at last we arrived at the end of
our resources and decided we must stake all upon
an invitation to camp with us, and so we rode a
little to one side of the trail, dismounted, and
unpacked enough to indicate our intents to the
mystified John. We then invited him by quite
unmistakable signs to honor us by camping with
us. To our surprise and joy he accepted.

That night Andy originated his famous game
of "outnizzening the nizzen." *Nizzen* is the
Navajo expression for "Do you want?" The
rules of the game are quite simple. Implements
consist of food and a Navajo. Any kind of either
article will do, and the plural of the first is ac-
ceptable or the plurals of both. Point to the
food, look at your Navajo, say "Nizzen?" If you
can say "Nizzen?" without his replying "Au"
(yes), you win. There is no case on record
where it has been done.

From John we obtained many valuable addi-
tions to our camping technique. It was a revelation to us to watch him make his bed. Our process was as elaborate and complicated as the
ceremony of making ye king's bed in ye olden

days: we examine with the aid of the light of a firebrand all the ground within a half-mile radius of our camp; as none suits, we come back to the fire, and I make my bed on one side and Roy on the other. I will not weary the reader with an explanation of our "systems" for arranging sheep-pelts, blankets, tarpaulins, and slickers. John had a much more efficient plan: with the help of a stick he smoothed the ground until *it* suited *him;* he then spread a blanket out on this space, placed his saddle for a pillow, lay down, drew another blanket over him, and in an instant was asleep.

In the morning we were awakened by John, singing his sun-greeting song: [1]

> Now the Mother Earth
> And the Father Sky,
> Meeting, joining one another,
> Helpmates ever, they.
> > All is beautiful,
> > All is beautiful,
> > All is beautiful, indeed.
> And the night of darkness,
> And the dawn of light,
> Meeting, joining one another,
> Helpmates ever, they.

[1] The translation is by Natalie Curtis.

All is beautiful,
All is beautiful,
All is beautiful, indeed.
Life-that-never-passeth,
Happiness-of-all-things,
Meeting, joining one another,
Helpmates ever, they.
Now all is beautiful,
All is beautiful,
All is beautiful, indeed.

The course which our friend took the second day was so entirely at variance with the one laid out for us by the trader that we were inclined to wonder if our comprehension of the Indian tongue was as correct as we had fancied. Before we could decide upon any plan of action, however, we were picking our way through a dense growth of underbrush. For the rest of that day and the next one it was interesting for us to speculate on exactly whither we were going. Our compass told us that we were going in a southwesterly direction, and we knew for a surety that we were going to that place to which John was going. We often met other Navajos, but never one who spoke English or Spanish and could thus enlighten us as to our whereabouts.

But as the weather was fine, the grass excellent, and the water-supply satisfactory, we were not greatly perturbed. On the morning of the fourth day we spiraled down a black hill, crossed a muddy stream, circled the base of a jutting hill, and then joyfully glimpsed a real windmill and a group of buildings at the base of a cliff. Conjecture was thus ended, for it proved to be the famous Chin Lee.

Chin Lee means in Navajo "where the water comes out." This name is applied to the trading-store and Indian school located near where the Rio de Chelly emerges from Cañon de Chelly. Here John bade us farewell; it appeared that Chin Lee for him was but the end of a leg of a longer journey. It was a mile-stone for us also, for our arrival at Chin Lee marked the end of approximately a thousand miles together on horseback.

We enjoyed a pleasant evening in the company of Dick, a government windmill tender, and three young girls who were teaching at the Indian school. The girls were receiving the munificent sum of sixty-five dollars a month for forsaking their own kind and coming a hundred miles from the comforts of civilization to teach homesick Navajo children. They explained to us that the doctor we had hoped to find had relinquished his post, feeling that he could obtain elsewhere better recompense than the princely salary of twelve hundred dollars a year paid him by the government. It can be readily deduced that this condition, coupled with the many disadvantages of location, hardly attracts the best professional material to the service.

XVIII

ONCE again we deviated from a strictly westward trail; this time it was to go up Cañon de Chelly. At its mouth at Chin Lee, the Chelly is perhaps a mile wide, and its sheer walls of purple sandstone are not more than one hundred feet high. Rio de Chelly, a typical desert stream, flows down the cañon. At the time of our visit, recent rains had swelled the little stream, which is almost dry at times, to a river of some proportions. This made travel difficult and, on account of the quicksand, a little dangerous. We followed rather carefully the tracks of a party of Navajos who were perhaps half a mile ahead of us.

As one traveled eastward, the Chelly rather seemed to shrink; that is, it grew more narrow, and its walls grew proportionately higher. A narrow, winding, water-worn, sand-covered floor between ever rising walls which allow no escape for a distance of forty miles; at various spots, the cañon widens a bit, and at these places corn-patches of vivid green, peach-glades. melon-fields, grass-hummocks, and reed-thickets contrast with the red walls and brown sands. Invariably a *hogan* and a flock of sheep or goats would dominate these cañon oases. About four miles from its mouth the cañon forks; there we left the Chelly proper to go up Cañon del Muerto, its principal branch. Cañon del Muerto gets its gruesome name from the massacre of Navajos there by the Spaniards in 1804.

For two days we traveled up Cañon del Muerto until we reached a place where further progress was too much of a hardship for our horses. As there was no break in the perpendicular walls of red sandstone or other possibility of egress from the cañon, we were forced to retrace our steps.

We had made many vain attempts to dispose of Babe, for she seemed to be gradually weakening, and on two occasions we had almost lost her in the quicksand. Several times we seemed to be making good progress toward a trade until we told the owners how much boot we would give them. We usually started with a dollar or two and stopped at ten. But when we mentioned *nack ee do clish,* which we thought meant ten dollars; they invariably laughed or became somewhat indignant and left us. When we returned to Chin Lee we learned from the traders that *nack ee do clish* meant twenty cents.

In Cañon del Muerto we obtained a picture of primitive Navajo life as it has been lived for centuries. In the level floor of the cañon the Navajos have their corn-fields, encircled by rude fences of brush, where by the crudest of methods they produce enough corn for their own use. Side by side with the corn-fields are the peach-orchards; the Navajo peach is a small but extremely delicious fruit. The only other crop of importance is that of melons. Indians of the Southwest are ravenously fond of all fruit but particularly of melons, and they raise watermelon, muskmelon, and what they term winter melon, a hard type of fruit which keeps well. Agricultural conditions are particularly favorable in Cañons del Muerto and de Chelly, for the overflowing of the streams furnishes an imperfect sort of irrigation.

The principal industry in these cañons as

everywhere is that of sheep and goat raising, for those animals furnish the Navajos with their principal means of subsistence. From them they obtain meat; they obtain milk from the goats; they sell the mohair and wool; and they obtain the wool for the making of their blankets and rugs. Early in the morning the children, assisted by dogs of every description, take the herds from the *hogan* to some place where the ruminants may find a little stubble. It is remarkable what the animals can live on, yes, thrive on. The youngsters seem to enjoy their occupation regardless of weather and other distractions; they sing almost continuously.

If the word "Navajo" has any general association in the American mind, it is with rug-making, which has become the principal and distinguishing industry of the Navajo nation. It was in Cañon del Muerto that we became familiar with the background and the step-by-step development of these rugs, which are now represented in virtually every community of size in the United States. When the time comes to shear, the flock is driven to the nearest stream, and there a temporary encampment is made while the whole family participates in the shearing of the sheep and the washing of the wool. Then the women, with the most primitive of instruments, card and spin the wool against the time when they shall be established for a sufficiently long period to justify setting up the rectangular frame of native cedar, rough and unfinished, which serves as loom. To the upper and lower bars of the rectangle the squaw ties the warp, weaving in the woof with swift deft fingers, stopping as she finishes each row to pound it tight with a stick. From the finished rug one may imagine much of the character and life of the weaver, in the same fashion that the home of an American housekeeper reflects her personality: if the rug is loosely woven, if the edges are not even, if the wool is not clean, if the black and white have been carelessly carded together to form the gray, if the patterns are not geometrically correct, one may rightly infer that the rug was woven by a dowdy shiftless squaw.

When the Spaniards first entered the Hopi villages in 1540, they found the Hopis growing cotton and weaving it into various articles of apparel, but their nearest neighbors, the Navajos, at this time did not weave, but stole their woven articles in raids against the less powerful Hopis and Zuñis. Navajo tradition has it that, after the coming of the Spaniards, Zuñis and Hopis instructed the Navajos in the weaving of cotton and also in weaving the fleece from the sheep which the white invaders had brought. These first rugs were woven from wool in the natural colors of white, black, gray, and brown, and from mineral and vegetable dyed wools. Red dye was obtained from the bark of tag-alder and mountain mahogany and from red ocher; yellow from various flowers and yellow ocher; black from twigs and leaves and from charcoal; blue from indigo, which was introduced by the Spaniards; green from a combination of the natural yellow with indigo.

Collectors distinguish between three eras in Navajo weaving. The first period lasts until about 1875 and includes the famous *bayeta* blankets (*bayeta* is Spanish for flannel), which were first made from threads unraveled from Spanish uniforms; but from 1850 to 1875 this material was imported from Barcelona by merchants in Santa Fé, New Mexico. The buck, squaw, and saddle-blankets, squaw dresses, dance aprons and belts, hair and legging ties, of this *bayeta* weave are to-day of priceless value, both on account of their historical significance and from the fact that they were produced to last for ages, to be heirlooms, and are, in consequence, real works of art.

The rugs of the second period were made partly from old weave materials and partly from various manufactured yarns; while the rugs of the third period, which begins about 1885 and extends to the present time, have been produced in more hurried fashion for market demands, and are colored principally with aniline dyes, with the exception of those rugs that are in the natural colors of the wool.

It is said that no two Navajo rugs of exactly the same size, pattern, and color have ever been found, although rugs of similar design are often seen. This is not unnatural in view of the fact that the squaw weaves, as fancy dictates, the sacred symbols of the powers of nature, the objects of everyday life, or figures suggested to her by incidents occurring during the making of the rug; preconceived pattern or design she has none save what is in her mind. There are conventional representations: the cross represents the four cardinal points of the compass and also good fortune; there are the zigzag symbols for the male and female lightning; the bow and arrow, the corn-stalk and ear, animals, the sun, moon, and stars, rain- and sun-clouds—these occur commonly in recognizable representations. Arrangement of these figures in certain orders may relate a legend or myth. The colors have a significance very much like that which they have to us: red—bravery, joy, strength; blue—honesty, fidelity; black—sorrow, command, obedience, respect.

Rug-making may be said to be essentially the industry of the women, while working in silver is a common occupation of the men. From Mexican dollars furnished them by the traders, the silversmiths hammer out rings, bracelets, belts, earrings, necklaces, of intricate, startling, and unusual design. Much of this jewelry is set with turquoise, which for unknown centuries has been mined and prized by the races of the Southwest.

The remnants of the homes of a prehistoric people were a source of great enjoyment to us;

we often risked our necks in attempting to reach them, and when we did succeed, we horrified the Navajos by excavating a bit and proudly exhibiting the skulls and arrow-heads which we unearthed. One is inclined to wonder if it was not a winged race that held these cliff refuges which nestle in the crevices along the precipitous rock walls of Cañon del Muerto.

One day a storm arose with true Southwestern swiftness: at ten in the morning we were sweating from the scorching heat of the Arizona sun, but at eleven we were shivering in a cold rain. This rain seemed to have a decidedly bad effect on Babe; she gave every indication of being about to drop from under Andy. Presently we encountered a party of Navajos who appeared to be equipped with good ponies; they were going to their *hogans* some distance up the cañon. By a combination of words, signs, and facial contortions, we managed to convey the idea that we wished to exchange Babe and a sum of money for one of their horses. After considerable bargaining, in which we came off second best, Na Deen came into our possession. ("Na Deen" is the Navajo term for the fifteen dollars involved

in the transaction.) Thus we traded horses in
Cañon del Muerto, in a driving rain, beside roaring waters, and under dripping walls, with a gentleman who did not understand our language,
and whose language we did not understand. Well,
at any rate, the deal gave Andy much satisfaction, for Na Deen, young, frisky, sturdy, was a
pleasant change from weak, tallow-legged Babe.

The rain continued, but we were sure that it
would stop at any moment. "It never rains in
Arizona," we had been told, and accordingly we
did not accept invitations to stop in *hogans*. In
the late afternoon, just as we were entering a
narrow place in the cañon which was deserted at
that time by the Navajos, the persistent but
drizzling rain changed into a cloud-burst, the
water rising with such suddenness that we realized we must take refuge or our horses would be
swimming. But where? The cañon floor was almost perfectly level; the water was rising everywhere without discrimination. There were no
hogans. In the nick of time we descried a cave a
little above the level of the cañon floor, and in a
short time we were safely shivering under its protecting walls, with our horses hobbled at a place

where the water was only six inches deep. It was not too comfortable a night for us, for we were wet to the skin, and the lack of a fire and of warm food did not help matters at all. Another cause of some discomfort was that sheep had been the last tenants of the place, and they had left rather odoriferous reminders of themselves.

It rained all night. In the morning our horses were standing, helpless, in water a foot deep, while the water already creeping over the floor of our cave warned us that we must discover a better haven if we wished to prevent our belongings from floating away. We shed our garments and had an icy swim. We soon noticed what we had not observed the night before, a cliff-dwelling, untenanted, directly above our cave, which we could possibly reach with the aid of our ropes. I was elected to do the human fly act, for Roy's well known Shiprock fingers would not yet bend, and at last I clambered over the wall of the cliff. It was then fairly simple to transfer Andy and the contents of our packs. Having completed our moving, we escorted our horses to a somewhat better location. By this time the rain had stopped, but travel was not yet to be thought of. Another swim of exploration disclosed to us a Navajo fence, most of which we carried back to our dwelling, and by extracting the hearts of the logs we produced a smoky fire that cheered our spirits.

Again it rained all night, and we had visions of a good many things, but the blessed sun of the next morning showed our horses weary-looking but alive and safe. We were marooned in our cliff palace another day, the greater part of which I spent struggling with and cursing my boots, which I had foolishly removed while wet. I broke our cooking-spoon while using it as a shoe-horn.

It was with some misgiving that we started down the now trailless and trackless cañon, but we were impatient enough to be reckless. Our steeds plunged and stumbled but did not fall, and we reached Cañon de Chelly without mishap. A little distance up Cañon de Chelly Henry and I were leading the way across a perfectly safe-looking spot when I suddenly felt Henry's legs sinking under me. A few seconds later I was safe on a fairly secure piece of ground thirty feet from Henry. I do not know exactly how I performed the maneuver, but Roy says that I yelled, climbed to the top of the saddle, and jumped a clear thirty feet. I was quite alarmed enough to do all that. Henry struggled but kept sinking. Just in time, Roy put a loop around his neck, and we fastened the other end of the rope to the horn of the saddle on Lee-Lee, who nobly dragged him out. Henry and also my saddle and appurtenances were sad to look upon. We decided that enough was enough and pitched camp immediately, but the next day the Navajos resumed travel, giving us assurance of a trail to follow.

Cañon de Chelly has most of the essential characteristics of Cañon del Muerto, although the coloring of the rock is of lighter shades for the most part. Cliff-dwellings are equally numerous, and Casa Blanca (white house) was larger than any ruin we had seen in Cañon del Muerto. There are many strange natural formations in Cañon de Chelly—a window makes a perfect frame for the cañon a thousand feet below; there are several monuments of great height, and of these El Capitán stands supreme, for it is a perfect granite shaft towering skyward sixteen hundred feet; there is another monument which when viewed from a certain angle bears a distinct resemblance to a Chinese woman. In upper Cañon de Chelly we saw countless bear tracks, and one day we saw a little black fellow disappear in the timber.

One day, as we were returning toward Chin Lee, we noticed a great deal of activity among the Navajos: great numbers of them, all in festal array, were coming down from the upper cañon; some carried butchered goats or sheep; many had packs of peaches or melons. We were very curious, but our command of the language was not sufficient to enable us to understand the explanations they volunteered.

That night we had been asleep for more than an hour when we were awakened by the beating of many drums. A moment later a horrid yelling, which soon changed into a melodious song, echoed and reëchoed in the cañon. There was quiet again, and then a noise which sounded exactly like the yipping of many coyotes. Peace once more, but there could be no sleep nor peace for us. We had heard much of the mysterious beauty of the religious rites of the Navajos, and the fact that it was said that they did not look with favor upon white spectators only enhanced the appeal.

We slunk down the cañon, keeping under the protecting shadow of the cliffs, and in fifteen minutes we reached a place from which we could see a great fire with several hundred Navajo men wrapped in their blankets standing around it. Near-by were scores of smaller fires. The singing began again—weird melodies which reflected and portrayed the strange spirit of the desert; shrill fitful voices intoning the call of the hunted; then a deep, snarling, vibrating prelude to a swinging melodious chant.

Suddenly the whole scene was flooded in the unspeakable glory of the Arizona moonlight. We were seen; they called to us. Was it in anger? We brazened it out. When we approached the camp-fire they came to meet us and ˙offered their hands. They then took us to one of the smaller fires and fed us fruit and roasted meat. We remained all night, and before morning we sang some of their songs with them; this afforded them the greatest amusement, why we did not exactly realize at the time.

Back in Chin Lee, Father Leopold of the Franciscan Mission explained to us the significance of the "sing": it was a preparation for the

three-day squaw dance which was to begin west
of Chin Lee the next night; in the olden days
these rites were a war ceremony, but now they
were a part of the courtship of the young Navajos, and only young unmarried men who wish
wives participate in the pre-squaw dance "sing."
We decided to go to the squaw dance.

XIX

THE TRAIL TO TOD-A-NES-JE

W E had no trouble in finding our way to the scene of the dance, for all roads seemed to lead there; we passed and were passed by hundreds of Navajos on foot, on horseback, and in wagons. At last we came within sight of a hill that was black with a thousand Navajos and their horses. We stopped and made our camp, as we did not care to have our horses mingle with, and perhaps become lost among, the countless hobbled Navajo ponies which surrounded the camp of the Indians.

Darkness fell, and myriad fires blazed on the hill. We wrapped ourselves in our blankets, Navajo fashion, and tramped across the sage to the fires. Such a gathering! Probably fifteen hundred Navajos of all sizes and descriptions were come from all corners of their reservation; for the dances and religious ceremonies of the Navajo Indians constitute their social world, and they think nothing of putting a few belongings in a wagon or on a horse and riding or driving a hundred miles to a festivity where they will meet their friends and relatives and can discuss clan and tribal questions. When we arrived, supper was not yet over, and the smell of broiling mutton and of roasting corn was in the air.

At length the crowd assembled in an immense circular inclosure formed by a wall of saddles piled four deep. There was a great deal of animated discussion among the various groups, and then all was quiet when an old man arose to speak. When he finished, the chatter was resumed, and many seemed to disagree with the burden of his talk. A magnificent figure of a man, wrapped in a striking purple blanket, spoke at some length, giving way to a violent little person who harangued the crowd without much encouragement. We sought out a young Navajo who had the appearance of a school-boy and asked him in English what it was all about. Somewhat to our surprise, he replied in our tongue and told us that an Indian girl had been lost that afternoon in the quicksand of Cañon de Chelly, and that some of the elders were of the opinion that the dance ought to be postponed out of respect for her parents. We were considerably disappointed, but needlessly, for an hour later it was decided that the proper thing would be to go on with the dance.

Just as the moon arose, a large group of young men began a low-pitched chant to the accompaniment of the beating of many tom-toms. Gradually the pitch grew higher and the chant louder, until finally it was a chant no longer but a deafening shouting. This suddenly ceased, and all was very still. Then through the opening in the circle marched a double row of Navajo maidens. When they were all within the inclosure, the beating of the drums began again, and likewise a low chanting. The girls separated; each found a partner among the young men and led him to the center; the dance was on. There was nothing very startling or complicated about the movements of the dance; indeed the figures were reminiscent of those of our old-fashioned country-dances. Some of the maidens were very shy, and their mothers assisted them in selecting their partners. Perhaps every fifteen minutes the music ceased, and some of the girls relinquished their young men to find others, but some kept their partners for long periods. It seemed customary for a young man, when released, to make some sort of a present to his lady fair. A good time was had by all, by the spectators as much as by the dancers.

There came a time when a maiden approached me, seized me by the arm, and drew me into the dance. A little later I saw Andy being madly whirled around. We were never sure whether, wrapped in our blankets, we had been, in the semi-darkness, taken for Navajos. But be that as it may, Roy and I danced the night long with aborigines in the light of the glorious Arizona moon.

During an interval in the dance, we crouched around a fire with a pleasant young Navajo.

"Ow goesh ya?" he said. This expression, meaning "Where are you going?" is used by all the Navajos; it seems to be a corruption of the English.

"Kayenta-go," we replied.

"Kay-en-ta—Dinne hasn Tod-a-nes-je." (Kayenta—the Navajo calls it "where three springs come out of the side of a hill.") Nonnezoche Not-se-lid dotsi? (Perhaps you are going to the Rainbow arch of stone?) And with his hands he formed an arch. Then he began to speak rapidly, eloquently. We only caught an exact phrase here and there:

"Ah, the Rainbow arch of stone . . . far, far in the bleak land where dwell the departed spirits of our . . . ancestors . . . but it is beautiful, beautiful . . . after the rock and the hard rock, to see Nonne-zoche, it is like the passing of the dark cloud when you lie in your *hogan* sick with desire of the sun . . . but it is long and it is hard, and you may never see again the dew drip from the tasseling corn . . . Astan Zoche will help . . . like the rainbow in the father sky, like the rainbow."

We caught but a phrase here and there to translate, but we understood, and at sunrise we started for Tod-a-nes-je. For nine days we saw no white men, nor even Indians who spoke English. We had no reliable means of finding our way, for signs there were none; roads were few; there was a multiplicity of trails, but they were merely added to our confusion. From our compass we took a northwesterly direction and followed it as closely as possible; in addition, we asked the Navajos many times each day, "Had-ish Tod-a-nes-je?" (Where is Kayenta?) Our best guide, however, was the fact that we knew that we must always keep the Black Mesa on our left. We were in sight of this immense plateau for a hundred miles of our way to Kayenta.

These were pleasant days, for although we did not know exactly where we were, we had plenty of food and water for ourselves and horses and a pleasing variety of experiences. Back in civilization, it seems rather strange how little it took to make our days in that primitive world so full and so happy.

We enjoyed the friendship of the Navajos, camping with them or being their guests in their *hogans* nearly every night. The Navajos were particularly hospitable and companionable. In fact, we found it a general truth that the farther away a Navajo is from a trading-post, school, or other influence of the white man, the better sort of fellow he is, for those close to the atmosphere of civilization realize too well the value of money. We were surprised to find that the Navajos we met each day always knew considerable about us: where we were going; how long we had been on the reservation; how we had treated their brethren. The Navajos are great gossips; news travels across the reservation with almost incredible speed. A trader, 175 miles from a white settlement, told us that he heard of the death of President Harding from the Navajos forty-eight hours after it occurred, although he did not receive his newspapers confirming the report until two weeks later.

We found much to admire in the Navajo character and customs. In some respects our race would suffer from comparison. I do not mean to idealize these Indians: our general conclusion was that they were very much like any other people; some are good, some are bad. They lack much of our knowledge, but they also lack many of the vices which we have developed along with that knowledge. We especially liked the Navajo family life; uniformly every one seemed contented, agreeable, and helpful. An unusually affectionate relationship exists between children and parents. Navajo mothers and fathers would seem to be more like older brothers and sisters to their offspring than stern parents. They give many privileges to their children; in fact, the children get the best of everything; they also give them quite definite rights with regard to the disposal of their own possessions. Contrary to the usual belief about the downtrodden, overworked Amerindian squaw, the Navajo marriage is essentially a partnership, with the preponderance of advantage and of power on the woman's side.

Many of our traditional conceptions of the Amerindian were shattered. Both Andy and I retained our boyish illusions about Indians and feathers; we associated the two together. We were just a little disconcerted when we spent several months among the Navajos without seeing a feather head-dress or even a single feather in the hair. Then there was the matter of cleanliness. I had always considered the American aborigine as rather filthy. My contact with some of the Pueblo Indians tended to confirm this impression. But the Navajos, as a race, are not so at all. I have seen a Navajo woman wash her hands three times in the process of bread-making, when possibly I had made biscuits that day without having performed real ablutions for some time. An almost indispensable adjunct of every Navajo home is a bath-house, very similar to the *hogan* in shape, but smaller. A pit is dug inside, while around and above this is a sort of bench arrangement upon which the person bathing sits, while another throws into the pit rocks which have been heated in a fire in front of the house, and pours water upon the rocks. The resulting steam gives the effect of a Turkish bath. One remains in the sweat-house for perhaps half an hour, is rubbed with grease and herbs, and then is expected to run up and down outside until dry. It is all very pleasant except the last part, which is rather disagreeable on a frosty November morning.

The Navajos in this part of the reservation hunt to a great extent with bow and arrow. Their marksmanship and the power of their weapon are almost uncanny, and they kill game of every description, including bear. Bear, however, according to their superstition, should be avoided and killed only when absolutely necessary. The youngsters handle bows and arrows as soon as they are able to walk, and they are excellent shots before they are in their teens. The Navajos have a gambling game which is rather fascinating. A boy fifty yards from the contestants hurls a reed into the air, and the men wager sheep or blankets as to where the contestant will hit the reed. Not whether he will hit it, where he will hit it.

It takes no great outlay to begin Navajo housekeeping. A few skillets and pans, some pottery, some baskets, rugs, and sheep- or goat-skins, are the essentials of equipment. There is also usually a broom made of wild turkey feathers to sweep the dirt floor. As for provisions, the most you will commonly find in a *hogan* is a sack of flour, some hand-ground corn-meal, a package of coffee, some fresh meat, some dried fruit, and a little sugar. All household property belongs to the wife. The home is hers, and should she wish to divorce her husband she puts him out. The paucity of household goods is due in a large measure to the Navajo wanderlust. The Navajo does not care to remain in one locality very long: he loves to visit his relatives or to attend a religious ceremony; and also, if forage conditions are unfavorable, he must move his abode, that his sheep and horses may not suffer. In the summer the Navajo usually has no fixed residence, moving frequently with his flock, and erecting at night a brush shelter as a protection against the wind.

One night we were awakened by an unearthly moaning and shrieking which seemed to come from the vicinity of some fires we could see a mile or more to the west of our camp. At first we were content to turn over and attempt sleep, but at last curiosity got the better of us; and, after considerable difficulty, because of the arroyos with which the plain was gashed, we arrived at the fires. There we beheld a grisly scene: a girl, who had been struck dead by lightning three days before, lay prone on the ground; around her danced seven song-priests or medicine-men; they chanted weirdly; in the background were the relatives of the dead girl voicing their lamentations. We did not stay long. When the girl appeared to move, we felt that it was time for us to be going.

Many of the Navajo religious customs are beautiful and appealing, but they have strange superstitions with regard to their dead. They regard a corpse with horror and, as a rule, refuse to touch one. If a Navajo dies in a *hogan,* the *hogan* is sometimes pulled down over the corpse and burned; at other times the *hogan* is simply abandoned. We more than once met with grim and ghastly evidence of this custom. When possible, the Navajos remove a dying person to a shelter constructed at some distance from the *hogan.*

The scenery of the region between Chin Lee and Kayenta is typical of the Navajo Reservation. On the left, going toward Kayenta, always the strange and forbidding heights of the Black Mesa; elsewhere the wild beauty of the desert. There are purple gray distances of sage and grass; there are clumps of cedar and piñon cresting little hills; there are crag-environed buttes of passionate colors. It is a landscape in which noise, hurry, and disturbance have no place.

We saw few animals, tame or otherwise. There were occasional large herds of sheep and goats and horses; we saw a few Navajo cattle. Coyotes there were in abundance, and they were unsuspicious, too, for the Navajos seldom hunt them. Every night we had rather harsh music from a coyote chorus, and in the early morning hours we usually saw one or two slinking around our camp.

These were the only animals that appeared to inhabit the region, and of bird life there seemed to be none whatsoever.

Toward evening of the fourth day after the squaw dance we were traveling slowly down a valley amid the foot-hills of the Black Mesa when we suddenly came in sight of two buildings that were decidedly not of Navajo origin. For the past day the Navajos had been talking about a *nal ya ba hogan* (store), but we had assumed that they referred to Kayenta, which from location and description this group of buildings could not possibly be.

It was Chil-chin-be-toh (bitter-water-weed) trading-post. Mr. Dunn came out to welcome us with the cordiality which only the loneliness of the desert can beget. He took us into the house to present us to Mrs. Dunn and their two children. We were something of a curiosity. In six months the Dunns had seen but two white men; in a year Mrs. Dunn had seen only one white woman.

Mr. and Mrs. Dunn were dismayed when we announced our intention of proceeding. They would not hear of it. We were indeed glad that we accepted their invitation to remain, for the supper that Mrs. Dunn prepared for us could have been prepared only by a woman; it was a masterpiece of the culinary art, and I know that we showed our appreciation of it.

We talked until early in the morning. We were able to some extent to satisfy their hunger for a personal interpretation of the events going on in the outside world. For their part, they had much to tell that was vitally interesting to us. Both Mr. and Mrs. Dunn have a very sympathetic understanding of the Navajo, and they were able to give us entertaining and valuable information as to the character, mode of living, and customs of these Indians. One cannot but admire the fortitude which enables these traders not only to endure but also to enjoy such an isolated and solitary existence. Although a few times a year a government agent or a chance traveler happens in on them, their only real contact with the United States is through the mail, which an Indian brings from Kayenta once a week, weather permitting. This mail has probably taken a month in reaching Kayenta, weather also permitting. Every eighteen months they return to civilization for a short visit, but while at Chil-

chin-be-toh they are left to their own resources
for amusement and occupation. Trading with the
Navajos occupies the major portion of their
time; Mrs. Dunn is nurse and doctor to the Indians for miles around; books provide a never
failing source of enjoyment, and the whole family
devotes a large amount of time to studying the
customs and languages of the Navajos.

We refused to burden our friends with our
presence for the night. Instead we slept in a deserted *hogan* which the Navajos regard as
haunted. It may or may not be haunted, but I
should like to remark that it is not a cheerful
place to sleep when the wind whistles through the
cracks in the roof, and when one finds that the
sharp object which has been sticking into one's
back is a bone of some sort.

Instead of leaving Chil-chin-be-toh at sunrise,
as we had planned, we remained until noon dis-
cussing with Mr. Dunn the preparations we must
make at Kayenta for our proposed trip to the
Rainbow Natural Bridge. In the first place, the
Rainbow Trail is a long trail and a hard trail,
and we were in need of fresh mounts. We were
worried by the fear that we might not be able

to insure a good home to the faithful Henry and
our beautiful Lee-Lee, but Mr. Dunn simplified
this problem for us by saying that he would be
glad to buy Lee-Lee for his son, and that he
would send to Kayenta for her in three days. He
was extremely interested in our plans, but he
advised us by all means to hire one of the Wetherill guides, or at least a Navajo. We told him
that we had traveled close to fifteen hundred
miles on horseback without a guide and that we
rather disliked to hire one at this stage of our
trip; but he still urged us to secure one, saying
that the Rainbow Bridge trail is the most difficult
in the West, and, since men who knew the country and spoke good Navajo had tried and failed,
we could hardly hope to reach the Bridge unless
guided. Furthermore we might quite possibly get
lost and die of thirst or starvation.

Soon after noon, we started for Kayenta, but
by a roundabout way which first give us an ex-
cursion to the top of Black Mesa. It was well
worth while. We found Navajos living in more
primitive conditions than any we had heretofore
seen. They were the most hospitable and friendly
Indians we encountered—also the most curious.

Many of the children had never seen white men before, for no road leads to the top of Black Mesa, ascent being possible only on foot or horseback. This fact accounts for its almost complete isolation from the white man. We noticed a curious phenomenon among the Navajos of Black Mesa: many of them had curly hair, not wavy, as kinky as that of a negro. Our visit to Black Mesa was marked by most peculiar weather, which gave rise to many petty irritations; I remember one day on which rain and sunshine alternated all through the day. At noon it was raining so hard that we postponed our usual lunch of a can of soup. At two o'clock the sky was clear and the sun shone brightly. We stopped, turned the horses loose, and built our fire. Just as we poured the soup into the coffee-pot to heat, it began to hail. Our fire was put out, our horses stampeded, and we were made very uncomfortable. Roy was human enough to curse.

Memories: Morning! Sandy, sagy flats—thickets of piñon and cedar. To the left, densely wooded Black Mesa, which is now terminating in a spear-point; to the right a continual procession of chunky pink cliffs with fluted skirts like those of Navajo women; directly in front sentinel shafts in warm shades. The usual day: Riding, just riding along. Night: Camp at the base of a mesa, one log for a fire, shrill whoops, a black and white baa-ing stream passing, Navajos waving greeting, an inquisitive coyote circling the camp, the bell tinkling obligato to the coyote chorus. Morning: An early start. Will we never reach Kayenta? Mr. Dunn said it could not be seen from a hundred yards in any direction, but we surely should have been by this time vouchsafed that advance glimpse which one usually gets on the desert. We followed directions implicitly and should have arrived before this. A *shi-dez ya* (sister) on a burro. "Ha dish Tod-a-nes-je?" (Where is Kayenta?) "Cugee!" (Right there!) A dirty look for kidding us, we ride on fifty feet, and drop into a slight depression containing a rambling stone house, trading-post, corrals, a windmill—Kayenta.

XX

H I, fellows, my name's Jack Wade."
"And mine's Red! Welcome to our
city! And what can we do you for?"

"Is Mr. Wetherill here?"

"Nope. He's out in the Bridge country with
Zane Grey and Jesse Lasky, but here's Clyde
Colville, who's been his partner for a good many
years."

"How are you, Mr. Colville? Wonder if
there's any mail for us."

"I think there's a pretty good-sized package.
Come in the store. Here you are. You may not
realize it, boys, but you're getting mail from the
farthest post-office from a railroad in this U. S. A.
It gets here once a week, after a haul of a hundred and seventy-five miles from Flagstaff. The
next nearest post-office is Tuba City, seventy-
five miles off. Well, there's Fanny ringin' the

dinner-bell, so you better let your mail go and come with me."

We were hardly prepared for what we found in the Wetherill residence, which adjoins the store; we expected a frontier house with frontier furnishings, and the exterior of the house is not extraordinary, although it is surrounded by the first real lawn we had seen on the Navajo Reservation, but Andy and I contend that the interior of the Wetherill home is one of the most attractive in America. The living-room is cheerful and inviting, with its huge fireplace surmounted by replicas of gorgeous Navajo sandpaintings, its floor covered with unusual rugs, its walls hung with rare blankets and Indian handicraft of every description. But we were to have yet a greater surprise: when we were told that we would be taken to a bath-room to wash, we expected the conventional desert wash-basin, bucket, and soap, but here in Kayenta, Arizona, last outpost of civilization, we found a bath-tub and running water!

Having made ourselves somewhat more presentable, we started for the dining-room, but even our usually invincible appetite was insuf-

ficient to cause us to hurry there, for in the hall
was another startling collection of wonders. In
addition to many objects of historical interest
and many articles of Navajo or Hopi Indian
workmanship, there was a veritable art gallery
—cartoons signed by Herriman, Dirks, Smith,
Swinnerton, and many other famous contem-
porary illustrators and cartoonists; there were
also paintings bearing equally famous names.
The dinner-gong sounded again, rather imperi-
ously, and we reluctantly started once more for
the dining-room.

The Wetherill family—so it seems natural to
call them, although only two of the twenty-odd
persons bear the name—is seated at a long table;
between two Navajos, an old man and a youth,
with whom she is engaged in earnest conversation, sits Mrs. Wetherill, whom the Navajo for
twenty years have called Astan Zoche (the little
slender woman), although she seems neither little
nor slender, as she leans forward in her chair,
while succulent aboriginal phrases roll from her
lips not less easily than from those of her audi-
tors. She cannot seem slender now, since she is
quite frankly plump; and she does not seem little,

because those snapping black eyes, that definite jaw, which occasionally clicks shut, and the vivacity of her gestures suggest so much power, so much vital energy, that her relative physical size is obscured at first by the suggestions of power in specific characteristics. She wears a street-garb which might be worn by any American woman of middle age, and her straight jet hair is dressed after the manner of Los Angeles; but her face belies equally the daughter of the town or of the provincial farm, for not even her indubitable inheritance from Irish progenitors —the flash of the eye and the quick smile or determined pursing of the lips—can entirely obscure the lines which loneliness and longing have graven deep in her brow and in the furrows drooping from the corners of her mouth. The desert chasteneth whom it loveth.

Opposite his mother sits Ben Wetherill, strong son of the desert and true brother of the Navajos; his life has been replete with unusual and thrilling incident. Jim Swinnerton, the creator of "little Jimmy"; Mrs. Swinnerton; Mr. Bergdoll, an artist come to Kayenta for the colorings of the wild landscape; Mr. Colville; Jack Wade;

Red; Smith, a cowboy preacher; Lee Bradley,
an educated Navajo in the service of the Wetherills; two agents of the Indian service who
happened to be passing through Kayenta—these
completed the gathering.

That afternoon we devoted to caring for our
horses and looking to our correspondence. We
were disappointed to learn from our letters that
one of our Mesa Verde friends would be unable
to join us, but Doc was on his way to Kayenta,
and we might expect him on the next mail. We
signed our names in the guest-book. There are
few registers, I am sure, which contain the signatures of a greater variety of persons: Theodore
Roosevelt, the Duke of Westminister, Zane
Grey, and an astounding galaxy of the famous
of earth; but in numbers equally profuse are
the signatures of wandering cow-punchers and
prospectors.

We were unable to make definite plans for our
trip to the Bridge until Doc arrived, and so for
two days we simply enjoyed ourselves. We
loafed in the store watching the Navajos trade.
They are very particular and fastidious customers: they wish to be sure that they have the

best possible bargain before buying; and so they never buy more than one article at a time, but when they are finally satisfied about a particular purchase, they pay for it, and then wait for some time before they begin to select their next want. A Navajo trading-store has many institutions peculiar unto itself. One is free tobacco—the trader has on his counter a box of cut tobacco from which his prospective customers may help themselves; he places nails in the bottom of the box, however, so that it is not possible to take a very large amount at one haul. I should not care to trade at Kayenta, Arizona, for any length of time. The supplies must be hauled all the way from Flagstaff, and the freight triples and quadruples prices. Oats are six cents a pound; alfalfa, when obtainable, is seven cents a pound; canned fruits are sixty cents a can; sugar is twenty-seven cents a pound. Sugar is always high on the reservation. The traders explain that the Navajos resent any raise in the price of coffee, but they do not seem to mind a high price for sugar, and therefore traders often sell coffee at cost and make their profit for both coffee and sugar on the sugar.

We cherish the memory of our evenings at Tod-a-nes-je. The pleasant fire in the fireplace set the tone for the general atmosphere. All the cow-punchers and Wetherill employees gathered together with the family, the celebrities, the travelers, to enjoy much good-natured joking and often something of a rough-house among the punchers. And the tales that were told—the cow-punchers told of the fun and hardships of their life; Jim Swinnerton of many places and many people; Mr. Colville of interesting travelers who had come to Kayenta. But Mrs. Wetherill excelled as story-teller—all manner of interesting and thrilling experiences encountered while traveling on the reservation, curious customs of the Navajos, their wonderful legends. I can never forget the story of Pueblo Bonito, the mysterious city of the ancients, as it was told to her by the old men of Chaco Cañon.

We were especially interested in the story of the discovery of the Rainbow Natural Bridge. As early as 1900 rumors came to Mrs. Wetherill of a wonderful multicolored arch of solid rock, and finally she met Indians who had penetrated the rock fastnesses of the region and actually seen the marvel. She induced her husband to set forth in quest of this solid rainbow. Two expeditions reached Navajo Mountain, only to be turned back by mountains of stone which seemed insurmountable barriers to further progress; but in 1909 a party organized by Professor Cummings of the University of Arizona and under the guidance of Mr. Wetherill again reached this barrier. Here the Paiute Indian who claimed to know the way across failed them. Mr. Wetherill, however, refused to fail and sent for Nas Ja Begay, a young Navajo who was some miles away tending his grandfather's sheep; and Nas Ja Begay conducted the party over a trail of almost unbelievable hardship around back of Navajo Mountain to the Bridge itself. Professor Cummings was the first white man to look upon Rainbow Bridge, and John Wetherill the first to ride under its arch. Since then many have attempted the trip, but a large part of them, unused to the rigors of the trail, have failed, and comparatively few have written their names in the book underneath the Bridge. Mrs. Wetherill is one of the few women who have achieved the trip. Navajos do not like to visit the region of the Bridge; they believe that it is the abode of great spirits, and if the Navajo does go he will not pass under the Bridge without repeating a certain prayer; if he does not know this prayer he must climb over the arch.

Until recently the Rainbow Natural Bridge was easily the most inaccessible and least visited of the natural wonders of America, for the trip was long, toilsome, and dangerous; the traveler had to make first the long journey of a hundred and fifty miles to Kayenta from the railroad at either Gallup, New Mexico, or Flagstaff, Arizona, and there still remained a packhorse trip of more than a hundred miles over hard trails; consequently the complete time required for a visit to the Bridge was at least several weeks, and there was a considerable expense involved; the number of people, therefore, who could stand the trail, afford the expense, and give the time was limited indeed. It is not likely even now that Rainbow Natural Bridge will ever become a tourist's paradise; but, since Roy and I have returned to white man's land, Hubert Richardson, an Indian trader of Winslow, Arizona, has discovered an approach to Rainbow Bridge from the south and west and has accomplished what seemed to us an impossible task: he has built a road to within the very shadow of Navajo Mountain which is said to be passable for automobiles. And so, now, at greatly reduced expense, one may go from the railroad to Rainbow Bridge and return in little more than a week; and, in the five years that have elapsed between our adventure and the publication of this book, the number of those who have looked upon Nonne-zoche has tripled or quadrupled. Hundreds will see the Bridge where ten did heretofore, but it must be truly said that they will miss much of the thrill and many of the picturesque beauties of the old Kayenta trail.

We had many long talks with Mrs. Wetherill about the Navajos. She has spent thirty years among them and is one of the few of our race and the only white woman to be adopted into their tribe, being an honored member of the aristocratic Tol-chini clan. Every Navajo on the reservation knows of Astan Zoche (the little slender woman, although Mrs. Wetherill is no longer slender); they have learned that Mrs. Wetherill is their true friend, and they come great distances to seek her aid or advice, and her word is virtually law among them. It was most extraordinary to see them enter her house (the door is always open), come and shake hands with her, and sit by the fire to talk or just to listen.

If you hear Mrs. Wetherill talking with several Navajos you cannot distinguish her accent; she is one of few persons who really speak their language. The school-boy who curses the intricacies of Greek should be thankful that he does not have to study Navajo; for although the Navajos have no written language, their oral tongue has a perplexing syntax and grammar, and the thirty-six sounds of their alphabet are baffling. It is said that the Navajo vocabulary is as large as that of English; the more complex Navajo words, however, are made of simple root forms. The verbs are the most important words in the language; and if one exactly understands the verb in a sentence, one can guess the meaning of the complete sentence. Verbal conjugations are very complicated: there are three numbers, singular, dual, and plural; the third person of the verb has an additional form which might be called the augmented third; adverbial prefixes and suffixes are very confusing. Perhaps the most confusing aspect of the entire language is the presence of a number of class verbs whose form varies according to the nature of the object affected by the action of the verb. For example, the verb "to give" has fourteen different parallel forms according to the class of the object that is given. The class is shown by the termination.

Mrs. Wetherill corrected a good many erroneous impressions we had received from traders and Navajos regarding the Navajo religious beliefs. She warned us that but few traders gain any but a superficial knowledge, and the Navajos themselves can seldom be accepted as authority, for the younger men know but little and answer to be polite, while the older men will purposely give the wrong impression in order that white men may not have the opportunity to ridicule their beliefs. The Navajos have a beautiful and important mythology, and their code of living is based upon a religious philosophy and certain ethical principles. It is interesting to observe that they have a crude idea of the theory of the superiority of mind over matter and that many of their ceremonies are a practice of this theory.

Some of the Navajo superstitions are most interesting. We learned why the Navajos always refused to let us take their pictures. They, in common with most aboriginal peoples, feel that a picture is a reproduction of an individual and that when the reproduction is made the individual is robbed of a part of his being. They view with especial horror the taking of the picture of a pregnant woman. Navajos refuse to eat fish or any sea-food, for they believe that the eating of anything from the sea will cause white spots to appear on their bodies. Mrs. Wetherill thinks this may be an indication that the Navajos once lived near the ocean or possibly on the islands of the Pacific, for it is a well known fact that fish as a principal article of diet induces leprosy. We had learned that the Navajos seldom kill coyotes and certain other animals and birds. Mrs. Wetherill explained that a Navajo belief is that when a person dies the spirit goes to dwell in a deep cañon where every one is happy, but sometimes the inhabitants wish to go back to see what their friends and relatives are doing, and for this reason there are piles of coyote-skins and of owl-feathers on the edge of the cañon which any one may don when he wishes to go back to earth. The Navajos, therefore, fear to kill coyotes or owls, since by so doing they might be preventing one of their dead relatives from returning to the happy cañon and cause the spirit to wander forever on the face of the earth.

Mrs. Wetherill explained to us in detail the strict mother-in-law taboo which exists among the Navajos: a husband must never meet his mother-in-law or any of her sisters or her mother after marriage; they must never be in the same dwelling; they must never speak to each other; if circumstances arise that make communication absolutely necessary, one shouts to the other at a distance, using the third person. It is curious to see a man or an old woman hide in or run from a trading-store when warned by the sibilant hiss, "Nas ja," of the approach of mother-in-law or son-in-law. The penalty for the infringement of this taboo is supposed to be blindness. Most Navajos give no reason for this custom, simply saying that such intercourse is improper. Several of the old men, however, told Mrs. Wetherill that

the practice was originated long ago by wise men
who wished to keep the mothers-in-law from making trouble in the homes. It is worthy of remark
that this identical custom prevails among the
nomadic tribes of Mongolia.

It was our good fortune to witness, while at
the Wetherill home, a spectacle that is as interesting as it is uncommon, a Navajo trial. The
government administers justice among the Navajos by means which are not very definite and
perhaps not always just. The superintendents of
the various agencies are the supreme authorities
in their own jurisdictions, but to take care of
minor disturbances and disagreements they ap-
point Navajo policemen and judges, one of
whom presided at the trial which we saw conducted in the Wetherill living-room. The judge,
a middle-aged man of fine poise and dignity,
came in and, after paying his respects to Mrs.
Wetherill, seated himself in a chair in the center
of the room. The accused, a young educated girl
charged with disturbance and incorrigibility, was
brought in by the policeman and seated facing
the judge, while an old Paiute woman whom the
girl had mistreated was seated on the other side

of the room. The entire affair was conducted in an orderly and businesslike manner: the judge questioned the Paiute woman, and several others were called to testify to the unsatisfactory character of the girl; the judge then asked the girl if she had anything to say for herself; she was very sullen; Mrs. Wetherill was then asked for her opinion; Mrs. Wetherill spoke rapidly in Navajo, and there was much nodding of heads by those assembled; the judge in a stern yet kindly manner delivered a lecture to the girl and forced her to apologize to the old lady. The trial was over.

The mail came, and with it the word that Doc had been suddenly called to his home in California. We now had to make a difficult decision with regard to making the trip to the Bridge. We had heard so much of the beauty and fascination of the trip that we could hardly bear the thought of giving it up, and yet it was rather hazardous for a party of two to try it unguided. We asked Mr. Colville what the charge was for one of the Wetherill guides. He would make us a rate of ten dollars a day including guide, horse, and food for both. Ten dollars a day for twelve days! It would have to be just the two of us or not at all. We collected opinions on the feasibility of such an undertaking. The general verdict was: Don't try it; it is a hundred miles away through roughest of country and very little trail; you finally reach a region where there are not even any Indians; questions of water, food supply, loss of horses, sickness (three weeks or more from a doctor). Mrs. Wetherill was the only one who gave us any encouragement. She said that we were horse- and trail-broken at least, and that even if we did not find our way to the Bridge we could blaze a trail so that we could find our way back. This sounded reasonable, and the lure of adventure was long and our cash short, so that, as Roy expressed it, "The Boy Adventurers put thoughts of fear aside and set forth in quest of the Rainbow."

There were some preparations to be made. We needed two fresh steeds. We had already sadly watched Lee-Lee leave for Chil-chin-be-toh in the hands of Mr. Dunn's Navajo messenger. We bought a buxom buckskin horse from Mr. Colville to take her place, or, more truly, to perform her duties, for no living equine quadruped could ever take Lee-Lee's place in our hearts. But Henry remained to be disposed of. A whole day we spent trying to arrange a trade; but there were many difficulties, for few Navajo horses met our requirements as to character and physique; prices were hard to adjust; and many of the Navajos were unable to satisfy us of their fitness to assume the proprietorship of our beloved Henry horse. On the other side of the fence, many did not wish to trade; others wanted exorbitant sums to boot; a few dared to suggest that on account of his advanced years our Henry was not suitable to their requirements. In the late afternoon, a big, handsome, white horse carrying a genial young buck proudly pranced into Kayenta. "There," I said to Roy, "is the type of horse I want." Luck seemed to be with us: the horse was young and physically perfect; the man seemed to possess the required temperament; and he was willing to trade and did not require too much boot. Our horse secured, we bought what seemed to us sufficient provisions for an army for a year. We then made our wills and went to bed dreaming of horses and of grotesque arcs exhibiting the several colors of the spectrum.

XXI

KAYENTA individually bade us farewell; and we had a melancholy sense
that they felt that it might be "farewell"
rather than "till we meet again," for they seemed
to hold out only one hope for us, and that was
that we might meet the Zane Grey-Jesse Lasky
expedition under the leadership of Mr. Wetherill,
which had set out some weeks before to try to
reach Wild Horse Mesa, which lies north of Navajo Mountain, across the Colorado River.

It was an unpropitious day, raw and cloudy,
and dismal gusts of cold wind blew the sand in
our faces. Red, who was riding to Tuba, escorted
us as far as Marsh Pass, which lies between sullen Black Mesa and Combe Ridge. There he once
again went over the little map which he and Jack
had drawn the night before in the lantern-lit
store. A few more directions, some general advice, good-by, and good luck. We turned to our
right and took the trail up Segi Cañon.

The crumbling red and yellow walls of the Segi seemed strangely suggestive of the jaws of a monster opened up for its prey. The trail was terrible, having been badly washed by recent rains. The deep arroyo with its labyrinthine branches had to be crossed and recrossed. Up and down. Down and up. Up and down. Down and up. We seemed to make no progress. The white Navajo pony, which had gone well enough on the wagon-road, now needed to be spurred continually. A young Navajo overtook us, joined us, and led us along at a faster pace, indicating that there was good grass somewhere in the distance; but falling night and the now bitter cold forced us to halt on a poor grazing-site. Navvie proved his usefulness by dragging in whole trees for the fire. He then joined us in the good old game of *nizzen*. Yes, he had heard of Nonne-zoche Not-se-lid, but the spirit of his grandfather forbade that he should go there. He would vouchsafe no information of his destination or purpose in traveling; we guessed that he was in search of a wife. In place of his unpronounceable Navajo sobriquet, we called him John.

John brought us our horses in the morning and

then left us. The banks of the arroyo became
steeper and yet more steep. We invariably had to
dismount to go up them, and twice it was necessary to unpack Buck and carry his burdens. This
was not due to any lack of endeavor on his part;
indeed we were not long in discovering that Buck
was worth his weight in gold to us, for he was
extremely strong, sober, and trustworthy. We
shall not soon forget the toil of carrying the panniers up those perpendicular banks; they had
never been heavier, and the chill of the day before
was now supplanted by the usual overpowering
heat of the Arizona sun.

We moved slowly watching for the cañon to
fork. It took many side-trips and much search
and exploration to convince us that various little
indentations in the cañon walls were not forks in
disguise, but when we did arrive at the forks they
were sufficiently plain; the cañon split squarely
three ways. After some difficulty in crossing the
arroyos, for there was nothing that resembled a
trail to guide us, we reached a point from which
it was possible to travel up the middle fork. Several hours or several miles later, the cañon forked
again; this time it seemed to branch out toward

every point of the mariner's compass. This did not agree with our map at all, and we were at a loss to determine which was the proper fork for us to take for the trail leading out of the cañon.

There followed three hectic days of exploration. We wandered up and down each discoverable fork seeking *the* trail, for we felt that in finding it, molding ourselves into it by day, and sleeping on it by night lay our only chance to reach the Bridge. Tracks and trails in the cañon were numerous. We made an interesting and close study of them. Mule-tracks and the tracks of shod horses indicated a Wetherill party, for few Navajos own mules, and none shoe their horses. A mule's hoof leaves a magnet-like impression, and magnets they became to us. Oh, the agony of having our trails or ghosts of trails suddenly disintegrate into a thousand dubious indentations! Mule or wild horse tracks? Fresh or ancient? And how illusive the blazer became on rocky stretches!

Then we gave up the hunt for the trail and decided we would be content to find our way out of the cañon and trust that once in open country our compass would guide us to Navajo Moun-

tain. But there seemed to be no break in the perpendicular walls. Once we found an old trail
which led us half-way up the height and then
turned along the edge of a rather friable clay
bank and suddenly stopped around a corner. I
could not turn my horse around; I could not get
off; I had to back up. Now, that may be a very
easy process with a Kentucky thoroughbred, but
I assure you that it is not with an ill broken, stu-
pid Indian pony.

At last we came to realize that we must do
something soon or return to Kayenta, for each
day wasted deprived us of a day's emergency
ration. We built rather a poor imitation of a trail
up an old rocky wash, and after several trying
hours we had our whole outfit out of the Segi.
Our feelings as we gazed down upon the almost
orange-colored domes which form the wall of
Segi Cañon were quite comparable to those of
Balboa as he first gazed upon the Pacific Ocean.
Utterly exhausted, we made camp at once. A
little later we discovered unmistakable hoof-
prints of shod horses and mules. This discovery
added greatly to our peace of mind.

For a few days we had comparatively easy

traveling. That is, easy with regard to natural
obstacles to our progress, for it was decidedly
not easy to find our way. We attempted to hold
to the trail with the right kind of hoof-prints, but
it forked and reforked, and when the terrain was
rocky or dotted with small pebbles the trail was
extremely hard to pick. We had one afternoon
that was especially bad; the trail led through dry
sand, and the markings became nothing more
than beveled puffs easily confused with slight
drifts made by the wind. The tracks one by one
vanished. We scoured to the right and we scoured
to the left in an effort to pick them up again; we
located one, then two, followed them a bit, deviated, circled; finally a goodly number of magnets reassured us, and we joyfully followed them
over the backbone of a ridge. Just then John appeared from nowhere; he was the first human
being we had seen for some time, and we were
glad. John had a smoke on us and confided that
he was in search of a cow. He was much amused
at the deadly earnestness with which we watched
the trail; he offered to lead us by a shorter route,
but we grimly refused. That night John played
nizzen with us again.

The following day we made good progress, although we did spend one hour going over the ground on our hands and knees in search of the evidential tracks. It was a desolate stretch of country and entirely deserted by the Navajos, although now and then we passed abandoned *hogans*. Sage-brush valleys, sandy flats, rocky hills, sandy flats, sage-brush valleys—a continual succession.

The white horse was not all that I had expected. He resented the daily travel over rough trails, and it became necessary to spur him more and more, although at first I spared him as much as possible, walking a great deal myself. After he had several times performed his predecessor's little stunt of running when hobbled, however, and had demonstrated in other ways equally irksome that he could be quite lively when it pleased him, I speedily lost all sympathy for the animal. The changes which we made in the horse's name show how by degrees our estimate of him changed. Before riding him I determined to call him Comet; after riding him a day I decided on Lightfoot; after two days I felt that Steamboat would be more appropriate. A little later Andy suggested

the name which stuck—Dotsi, which is Navajo
for "maybe so"—maybe so he would carry me to
the Bridge and back, and maybe so he would not.

One night we were camped below a hill of some
proportions. We were eating a late supper when
we heard cries from the top of the hill. Navajos,
we thought, but a minute later we heard cries in
a tongue which was decidedly not Navajo: "Get
along there, Skeeter!" "Over, Rusty!" "Get in
line, Ramrod, you—" It was Jesse Lasky, the
moving-picture producer, with a party of friends
and Wetherill guides. Zane Grey, John Wetherill, and the rest of the party were a day behind.
They had not been able to reach Wild Horse
Mesa because of high water in the Colorado and
a shortage of supplies. We passed a fine evening.
It was an unexpected pleasure for us, since we
had not hoped to meet white men until our prob-
lematical return to Kayenta, and, as for them,
they had been in the wilds for weeks and were
all eager for news from Kayenta. That night
Kayenta, Arizona, 175 miles from a railroad, with
its population of seven, seemed to us the hub of
the universe. We found Mr. Lasky a delightful
man, quiet, unassuming, and a ready worker.

Before we parted in the morning they assured us that we were headed in the correct direction and gave us valuable pointers for continuing our journey. That day we made camp early in the afternoon and spent several hours in completing the notes and maps we had made of our journey thus far, for we meant to be able to find our way back to Kayenta even if we did not attain our goal. A number of times each day we placed stone markers or blazed trees. John graced our camp again that night and played *nizzen;* he seemed to, haunt us.

Not so long after sunrise the following morning we stood on the edge of a deep cañon in which the purple smoke was rising. Far, far below lay Indian corn-fields and *hogans.* Wisps of gray smoke from their fires floated upward to mix with the elusive purple mist which the sun seemed to draw from the purple and red cañon walls.

We located a rude Navajo trail and started down it. The descent was slow, toilsome, and terrifying for both ourselves and our horses. Perhaps a quarter of the way down we were astonished to hear the sound of many voices. We looked down: Zane Grey's party, ant-like in appearance, was beginning the ascent. The guides drove the mules, a score or more of them, ahead, while the others followed leading their saddle-animals. There was one exception to this rule: Mr. Grey's Japanese cook, a puppy in his lap, rode a small mule. The narrow trail did not permit of many niceties, but we had a chance to look at Z.G. and to shake Mr. Wetherill by the hand.

In Paiute Cañon we secured corn for our horses and, treat of treats for me, a watermelon. The Navajos and the Paiutes living in this cañon seem to enjoy an especially happy and undisturbed life. The Paiutes are a vanishing race; in a few years they will be completely absorbed by the Navajos.

Climbing out of Paiute Cañon is a long exhausting hardship. We felt sorry for Buck, but he puffed along nobly. Just at the top we discovered that we had suffered a real calamity in the loss of a canteen. Andy went back to search for it but was unsuccessful. We tried to tell our trouble to a passing Navajo urchin, but he failed to comprehend exactly what we had lost. Out of the cañon, we caught our first real view of Nat-sis-an, Navajo Mountain, symbolical of Navajo nature. It rises suddenly and unexpectedly out of a fairly level plain broken only by rock formations suggestive of exaggerated toadstools. Nat-sis-an from Arizona is black, bleak, and gloomy, enlivened only by some turret-like formations of red and white rock. It was small wonder to us that the Navajo will never go more than a half-day's ride upon the mountain; that is, he never wishes to let the sun set with him upon the mountain. They believe that Nat-sis-an is the residence of the war-god, of the thunder, and of certain spirits. There is a story, which Mrs. Wetherill feels may have some foundation, that there is on Navajo Mountain a crudely carved image of the war-god.

Another day, and we were a little to the east of the mountain at a Navajo settlement called *tsa hogan,* or "rock house," since one of the very few rock dwellings in the Navajo Reservation is located in this settlement. It was a very pleasant community, and we enjoyed spending the night there. They gently attempted to dissuade us from going farther; they said that if we entered the barren country on the other side of the mountain both our horses and ourselves would die from the heat, from thirst, and from starvation. They seemed sorry to see us go. It was a strange coincidence that on the morning when we said goodby to these, the last people we were to see for some time, both of our watches should stop.

Two days we spent in working round toward the north face of Nat-sis-an. At some time we crossed the Utah-Arizona boundary; the exact line in this region has never been surveyed; and at noon one day we reached the crest of one of the side-hills of Navajo Mountain. On emerging from a grove of trees we beheld before us a new and strange world: Rock, rock, rock; thousands upon thousands of red domes; more distant, two deep lines of red and purple; still farther away, snow-covered mountain peaks. The whole scene suggested a cubist painting. This region surrounding the cañons of the San Juan and Colorado Rivers is the least known and least explored area in the continental United States. The last stronghold of Virgin Nature!

XXII

THIS new world which we were entering seemed as an apparition, a mirage, an illusion. Could we be the victims of a distorted imagination, or had we been dropped upon or transported to a new planet? Accustomed as we had been to quaint perspectives, ancient ruins, phantasmagorial impressions of nomad life, mountain solitude, cañon depths, starry skies, and uninhabited wastes, this sudden view of a sea of gigantic, bare, iridescent, huddled planet tops, continuous as far as the eye could reach, was none the less appealing when we realized that within a short time we would have to find a path over these slippery monsters or turn back defeated. We found in this corrugated region many other changed conditions which made us feel that we were in another world; this feeling, in fact, was so complete that we began to call the region the Moon.

In the first place, the climate changed after we dropped into these cañons on the north side of Navajo Mountain: since leaving Paiute Cañon we had been waking up with a coating of frost on our beds, and except at midday it was never more than warm, but in or on the Moon it was totally different, for at night we slept under a single blanket, and in the daytime we soon took to riding shirtless. The atmosphere seemed entirely new; it had a peculiar reaction upon our olfactory organs. The vegetation changed too: grass had been short and scarce heretofore, but here it was green and luxuriant, waist-high; there were the rare orchid-like sago lilies—at first only the white ones; then as we dropped lower in approaching the level of the Colorado the delicate yellow and pink ones appeared, although they were no longer in their glory, but they were still things of beauty; the purple sage, which grows only in this region, was conspicuous, although it had long been out of bloom.

Each day travel grew more difficult; at times we traveled over solid rock for hours at a stretch. But again there were lovely valleys made verdant by cool brooks. Trail-finding was difficult;

we had to rely largely on our location with regard to Navajo Mountain; for our compass, for
some reason best known to itself, had ceased to
function. Now and then we would find some object which unmistakably indicated that a party of
white men had passed. How strange it was to
find an empty can or a cigarette-stub in that still
and silent void! As we penetrated farther down
the cañons and into the rocks, we found that
there was usually only one way in which it was
possible to proceed, and at first sight even that
way often looked impossible.

So it was when we came to Glass Mountain.
We had been following a trail that was fairly
plain, and other evidence had presented itself
that we were on the right track, when suddenly
loomed up before us great domes of bald rock.
A careful examination showed that there was no
passage between the slippery monsters; there was
no way around them, save for a bird. We were
disheartened at the thought of retracing our steps
many weary miles to seek a new trail, and so Roy
at the risk of his neck climbed to the top of the
first dome to get a general view. All of a sudden
there was a shout which indicated, I found, that

he had discovered a pile of horse-manure; a little later we were sure that the way lay not
through the domes or around them but over
them.

It took some little time to convince our horses
of this truth. Neither Andy nor I nor our horses
will ever forget that slow, tortuous, nerve-rack-
ing trip across the Hills of Glass. Two little Gul-
livers, we stood before the first of the huge great
rock hills in the Sea of the Planet Tops; dismounting, we began timidly the climb up to the
first ledge: a slipping sound of hoofs, the *whack*
of a rope, the encouraging "Come on, Buck," the
planting grunt of a horse dropping to another
shelf, a narrow eight-inch ledge around the edge
of a brown dome, the easy climb to the edge of
the next world, the slippery drop of one hundred
feet to the next secure footing, which was tested
first by sliding boot and skidding trouser seat,
the breathless negotiation by one badly scared
animal after another in charge of two panting
little men.

By going over the rocks on our hands and
knees we could discern little white marks made in
the soft rock by the nails in the shoes of the

Wetherill horses, and so we had another Ghost Trail. But we followed it. We followed it up cliffs so steep and slippery that we in our boots could not walk up them; we clung to our horses' necks with our hands and pressed our spurs into their flanks, while good faithful Buck followed without being led; otherwise we could not have managed. In one place we went across a ledge so narrow that our horses could not stand on it with their feet parallel, and it was quite a nice drop to the little cañon below. There again we clung to our horses' necks and prayed. My craving to take a picture of the spot almost resulted seriously. Much to Andy's disgust, I insisted that he and the horses should pose on exactly the narrowest portion of the ledge. I crept out on an overhanging rock to snap the picture, slipped, and rolled down the rock for seventy-five feet. Fortunately the rock was rather soft, but we had to waste some valuable time in getting me up again. Roy let his lariat down, but it only came half-way, and so he had to unpack Buck and tie the pack-rope to the lariat. Then long-suffering Buck, assisted by Andy, dragged me up safely. It was really rather funny, but in thinking about

it afterward I decided that it would not have
been the best thing in the world to break a bone
in that neighborhood, since it was three weeks, at
the very least, to a doctor, assuming that I could
travel and that we could find our way, and, if I
could not travel, an eternity more or less.

In the late afternoon we paused to rest on top
of a fairly level rock hemisphere. Na-Deen and
Buck lay down with us. What a world! Our
"moon feeling" was greatly accentuated. Rock,
rock, rock, everywhere. No vegetation, life of any
sort, nor even earth could be seen. The domes
changed color in the sunlight. Navajo Mountain
was no longer black and forbidding; it was now
a fantastic mass of lurid-colored rocks. The still-
ness, the intense sense of physical loneliness, were
overwhelming. The barrenness of this blasted region is terrible yet beautiful and wonderful. It
was a picture of primeval passion, upheaval, and
revelation frozen into despairing granite; they
say no man has ever returned from this trip an
atheist, and I believe it.

The thought struck both of us at the same time
that we must move; it was beyond us; the scene
was too much for a finite mind. We had but an-

other hour before we were all safely on the dirt floor of a cañon which seemed as the fold of a great old-rose-colored velvet carpet carelessly dropped by some deity. To us it was the Valley of the Moon. Our descent to the valley was not the least thrilling of our experiences; it seemed an almost perpendicular drop; our horses were forced to walk sideways, and several times they slipped a few feet.

A day of twisting down cañons whose walls bore evidences of prehistoric occupation. We speculated on how the inhabitants of these cliff dwellings had reached this secluded spot and why they had come. Up and out of one cañon and down into another. Trails steep, crude, and arduous, but trails nevertheless, it was plain to be seen. We were content.

At last, after an especially difficult climb, we passed between a very narrow opening and into a wide garden-like valley through which flowed an inviting stream. It was Surprise Valley made famous in "Riders of the Purple Sage" and "The Rainbow Trail" by Zane Grey. Entirely surrounded by upstanding walls of red sandstone, there are only two openings, both narrow,

one of which can only be attained after the stiff-
est kind of a climb. The valley itself is the green
and growing oasis of the desert of rock. There is
life there too. Birds—one wonders where they
come from—coyotes, and other small animals.
The coyotes are unafraid; two ran over my legs
as I was crawling out from under my blanket in
the morning. To camp we moved back to the
pass, in order to be able, we thought, to control
the movements of our horses, for they had been
wandering far even among the rocks, and we
thought it would be delightful to rest one night
undisturbed. And so we hobbled them and barred
the pass, but in the morning they were gone;
hobbled, they had jumped the three-foot fence
we had erected, but fortunately they only went
down into the valley proper.

Getting out of Surprise Valley was an exhausting perpendicular process. We then crossed
a plateau littered with peculiar black rocks. To
our left was a stone fish, excellently carved; above
towered rust-colored castellated rock pinnacles;
many miles away, but apparently much closer,
was Wild Horse Mesa. This immense table-land
runs fifty miles back into Utah; many scarce be-

lievable tales are told of it. We dropped off the
plateau by way of a precarious path into another garden, where oak shrubbery tore our clothing and impeded our progress. We climbed out
again, circled back to a sloping flat, headed several small cañons, and came to what appeared to
be the jumping-off place. The trail was unmistakable, or we should have discarded as absurd
the possibility of jumping down into the aperture
which lay before us. But down into this steep
and narrow declivity we went; the panniers on
Buck scratched the side, and the saddles were at
forty-five-degree angles. In several places we
thought for a few moments that Buck was going
to remain stuck in Hell's Hole. It soon appeared
that the hole was the head of a small cañon, and
gradually as we went down it widened, finally
joining another cañon. All the time we kept going down, down, it seemed, into the very bowels
of the earth. At last we rode into a cañon of imposing proportions. We felt with a thrill that we
must be in Nonne-zoche Boco (Bridge Cañon).
It was hard work picking our way down the bed
of the creek, which was formed of slippery painful rocks. The trail slipped through clumps of

willows and oaks; always it led around another bend in the stream; once it led across a ledge some twenty feet above the floor of the cañon; the waters murmured like weary voices; the acoustic properties of the gigantic overhanging caves magnified hoof-beat and our monosyllabic comments. Our horses stumbled and fell. Dotsi pranced along like a circus-horse, never noticing where he put his feet. We were forced to give up hope of reaching the Bridge that night, and so we pitched our camp under a high bank in the shadow of the purple cañon walls.

Although we were hungry, supper was entirely a canned one, as we hurried through it. Then we started down the cañon, hoping, before night fell, to catch a glimpse of the wonder we had come so far to see. Around the first bend in the cañon we saw it—Nonne-zoche Not-se-lid, the incomparable, the indescribable.

It was hard to believe that this thing was of hard cold stone. In the setting sun it was warm, radiant, glorious. We had heard so much of the Bridge, we had read Zane Grey's inspired description—in short, we were prepared for the disenchantment which the real often gives to one's dreams. But this sight was more than recompense for the hardships and dangers of the trail. It awed and thrilled us as a wonderful symphony or a painting from the brush of a great master. And more—for was this not the eternal handiwork of the Great Master?

We crept closer. We found that we had not realized the great size of the arch, for it is so wonderfully graceful and so perfectly proportioned that its beauty rather than its colossal size first engages the attention. One could place the Capitol under it, however, and then have considerable room. The width of the span is sufficient to allow several automobiles to travel abreast with room for a few bicycles between them.

Gradually the reds, the blues, the yellows, the grays, the purples, in the rock faded and blended into deepest ebony. It was night, and the Bridge, which in the sunset had symbolized the Glory of Nature, the Reward of Toil, and Vibrant Passion, was now majestic and omnipotent Eternity; all the mystery and immutability of Fate were typified in that blackest curve. The moon rose. Nonne-zoche lost its hardness and in the soft light was again wondrous and sylph-like—

Young Love, Dreams, Sweet Music, the Beauty of the Quiet Places.

For hours we walked and sat and looked. Hardly a word was said. At last we slept. At the foot of the Rainbow, we had not found the pot of gold, but content and happiness.

Sunrise was a miracle. And before the sun came into view, clouds above Navajo Mountain changed color with startling rapidity. The turrets of the mountain were illumined with mystic shafts of light. There was a strange moving of shadows. Then suddenly all was light. Nonnezoche Not-se-lid was once more truly the Rainbow Arch—Birth, Youth, Ambition. Not the misty Rainbow of the heavens, but the permanent, changeless, roseate Rainbow of Stone. Unmarred by the water, ungrieved by the wind, it will endure forever.

Under the Bridge in a metal case is a book in which those who have looked upon Nonne-zoche write their names. It is a very interesting document, containing something less than two hundred names, among them some rather famous ones. We were eager to list ourselves in this Hall of Fame, but posterity came very close to losing that invaluable record. When we left Kayenta we each possessed an ordinary wooden pencil; Andy also treasured one of the so-called ever-sharp variety, which he was forever mislaying. Of course by the time we reached the Bridge we had both lost our ordinary pencils, and we had virtually exhausted the lead in the other one in making our maps and keeping our notes. If we had had a pen I would have experienced no compunction whatever is using a little of Dotsi's blood, but we had no pen, and so we seriously considered cutting off Dotsi's tail and brushing our signatures in after the manner of the Japanese; we decided, however, that Dotsi was perhaps a trifle better than no horse at all, although I afterward came to doubt this opinion. After much effort, by holding the pencil vertically we were able to utilize the small bit of lead which remained in the end of the point.

How we wished that we might spend several weeks exploring in the vicinity of the Bridge! But already we faced a shortage in provisions; therefore we determined to compress a good deal of exploration into a single day. First we walked down Bridge Creek to where it empties into the already Grand Cañon of the Colorado. It was a two-hour walk and a rough one, but it was worth it. On returning to our camp we endeavored to scale the cañon walls with but indifferent success, and afterward indulged in a refreshing swim in one of the tank-like pools which are to be found every few yards in Bridge Cañon.

Early the next morning we set out for Kayenta. On account of being sure of our way, we made fairly rapid progress even in the rockbound country surrounding the Bridge, where we were forced to walk most of the time. There was one impediment to our speed, and that was Dotsi. He had stood the trip better than the other horses, because he was always too lazy to exert himself. He was still fat and sleek and could see no reason to hurry back to Kayenta. I have been acquainted with horses of varying degrees of stupidity and orneriness, but I wish to state that Dotsi is by far the stupidest, dumbest, ugliest, and most contrary horse that I have ever hobbled: in riding on the level ground Dotsi could not be urged out of an ambling walk; in descending an almost perpendicular rocky hill he would trot and prance like a circus-horse; one habit that he never changed was that of not pay-

ing the slightest regard to the ground underfoot
or to the direction in which he was going. I am
not cruel by choice or by disposition, but that
horse exasperated me. At first I simply spurred
him, but my spurs became blunt; I then used a
leaded quirt, but out of this I beat all the lead.
Dotsi throve, but Andy swore I lost ten pounds
that day. Finally we found that if I spurred
Dotsi and beat him continually on both flanks
with a rope, and if at the same time Andy poked
him from the rear with a stick, sometimes he
would move.

We reached the Tsa Hogan community without unusual incident. It was good to see the Navajos; we had gone for twelve days without seeing a human being other than each other. They
seemed glad as well as surprised to see us. One
of them brought us watermelon, fresh meat, and
corn, and would take no pay. We were glad for
the shelter of a *hogan* that night, for the wind
howled, and the temperature dropped low enough
to freeze the water in our canteens.

Between Paiute Cañon and Segi Cañon we
were lost several times, to our great disgust, for
we were now living on limited rations. But the

country was so open and so much alike that, even
without detailed notes and maps, it was difficult
to be sure of ourselves. After a little, however, we
discovered that we had a seemingly infallible
guide in Na-Deen. When we lost the trail or it
disappeared, Na-Deen would keep turning in a
certain direction no matter which one we chose.
Several times he put us back on the trail, and so
afterward we gave him his head when we were
in difficulty.

We were indeed glad to look upon the orange
turrets of the Segi again. We camped at the head
of the trail which leads down into the cañon. The
next morning we combined our remaining provisions into one grand mess, resolving that it were
better to have one good meal and starve all at
once than to have several small ones and starve
by inches. Seven potatoes, a can of roast beef,
some rice, a little macaroni, a can of celery soup
—we dumped the entire aggregation into one
kettle, and with the little flour we had left I made
some biscuits. Our sugar and condiments were
gone entirely, and when breakfast was over, our
packs were empty save for coffee and our emergency ration of two pounds of stick candy.

About noon we arrived at the second fork in
the cañon. There Mind staged a redoubtable vic-
tory over Matter. We knew that up the cañon to
our right was one of the greatest prehistoric ruins
in America; we also knew that if we visited the
antiquity it meant several extra hours without
food. After some deliberation, we decided to see
the ruin, in view of the fact that it might be our
only opportunity, while we optimistically felt
that we would yet have many opportunities to
eat. We were not very hungry at that time; our
breakfast still rested heavily within us.

Beta Ta Kin, the house on the side of the hill,
transcended in beauty and mystery any ruin we
had seen: it is set in a natural amphitheater which
would hold Trinity Church, in the side of a cañon
which, at the time of our arrival, was a riot of
color—the poplar leaves had just turned golden;
the oaks were bushes of flame; the spruces with
their ever beautiful green added variety of coloring. Roy remarked that it would be a pleasant
place to picnic: this remark was not well received, for we had nothing with which to picnic.

For supper we each had six sticks of candy,
our emergency ration. The same for breakfast.

We rode all of the next day, and we rode hard. In the late afternoon our hearts leaped as we climbed out of the Segi and beheld the two brown parallel ribbons which, after weeks of lonely trails, seemed to us a boulevard in civilization rather than a desert wagon-road.

Kayenta seemed as elusive and as far distant as a mirage, but just at dusk we suddenly found ourselves there. On our arrival a battle almost ensued; for the crowd, in their eagerness to hear our adventure, threatened to keep us from food.

Ah, that first night back at Tod-a-nes-je! Cheery white faces, women's voices, real food; the dogs asleep before the fire, the pleasantly strange mixture of culture and frontier, the joy of temporary relief from worry over the whereabouts of our horses, the knowledge that the trail would not vanish in the darkness.

XXIII

W E spent six pleasant days at Kayenta on our return there. We had hoped that John Wetherill would be at home this time, but he had left some days before to guide an expedition of the National Geographic Society under the leadership of Neil M. Judd, excavator of Pueblo Bonito—which expected to penetrate the unexplored country north of Nonne-zoche Not-se-lid.

Our departure from Kayenta was delayed three days by the disappearance of Na-Deen. Tired of paleface masters, the Wild called him to return to the *hogans* of the Navajos, or else he returned to visit the frail Navajo lady horse of whom he had become enamoured our last night in the Segi. Although all hands joined us in the search, he was not to be found. Since we could not afford to wait longer, and as the low state of our exchequer did not permit our buying another animal, we decided that we could take turns walking. Roy Rutherford, one of the Wetherill cowpuncher guides, was frankly horrified when we announced our purpose. He insisted that we take one of his horses either as a gift or loan. Quoth he, "Pay when you like or don't never pay, same to me; but nobody walks in this country." Again the Old West. But Ben Wetherill had a big buckskin horse he wanted delivered at Tuba City, and that offered a solution of our problem for seventy-five miles at least. Before setting out, I tried my best to dispose of Dotsi, but he could not be given away. And so with big Buck, and little Buck and Dotsi, we left Kayenta with many regrets at separating from the wonderful people who live there.

Just before we reached the famous head of the Segi Cañon we saw a cloud of dust, two perspiring ponies at a gallop; and a Navajo boy returned Na-Deen to his fond parents. We gave the boy an unused pistol and some cookies, and he called it square. Andy now rode Na-Deen and led big Buck. The road was large enough for our party; but as little Buck, who was packed, persisted in following Dotsi, ridden by me, and as

Dotsi chose the center of the road, it meant that big Buck must run beside the road, and his efforts to push little Buck over gave Andy fits of hysterics, especially as little Buck with his bulging pack-sacks full of good hard cans of food kept raking the large horse's flanks as he attempted to close in.

The second day out from Kayenta we entered the wonderful region known as the Painted Desert of Arizona. It was the closest approach to the Sahara type of desert that we had encountered. We had passed through small stretches of plain sand, but generally I have used the term "desert" in the broader sense to signify a more or less uninhabited barren and semi-arid region. The sand in the Painted Desert could never be called "plain"; in fact, it is said that thirty-five different colors of sand may be found in this region. We did not identify quite that many, although when looking down from a height upon the desert glistening in the sunlight it seems that there are countless shades of sand. The sunrises and sunsets on the Painted Desert are superb and unearthly, the clouds changing color with unbelievable rapidity.

Shortly after we entered the Painted Desert region, we first beheld the triangular San Francisco Peaks, one hundred and twenty-five miles away. They mark the location of Flagstaff, Arizona, and likewise the Santa Fé Railroad. They were snow-covered, and it seemed quite natural, for the lake near which we had camped the night before had several inches of ice on it in the morning.

Fifty miles from Kayenta in the heart of the Painted Desert region is the fortress-like structure which is Red Lake trading-post, so called from the uninviting sheet of rouged alkali water which it surmounts. Mrs. O'Farrell, wife of the trader, greeted us with this remark: "I hope you are not as tough as you look." At first we were inclined to be insulted, but after thinking it over we admitted that it was quite possible that we did look tough. Neither of us had had a hair-cut for three months; we had not been shaved for six weeks; our apparel was no longer new. But despite our appearance and the fact that Mr. O'Farrell was in Tuba, and she was twenty-five miles from another white person, Mrs. O'Farrell was more than kind to us. She invited us to their living-room and fed us. Warmed by her cordiality, we confessed to her what we had not had the courage to tell the Wetherills: we were broke. We now had sixty cents between us and three days' provisions, and unfortunately we could not hope to reach Grand Cañon and the telegraph in three days. We refused the proffered loan, but we had a load taken from our minds when Mrs. O'Farrell bought our somewhat disreputable 30-30 rifle.

Tuba City seemed a city indeed to us. It was by far the largest community we had entered since leaving Farmington; there must be at least thirty persons connected with the Indian Service in permanent residence at Tuba City.

From Tuba we journeyed eastward to visit the Hopi village of Moencopie. Picturesquely located on the rim of a miniature magenta-buttressed cañon, the village and inhabitants of Moencopie were not so different from those of the New Mexican pueblos—terraced adobes, narrow crooked streets, red pepper strings against the walls, colorful costumes and bobbed hair of Indians. The Hopis are great agriculturists; they make the desert produce fruit and grain in abundance. We did not feel, however, that they compared favorably with our friends the Navajos in attractiveness.

From Moencopie we headed toward the Grand Cañon. When we came upon the automobile road which the Harvey company has recently constructed, that their patrons may view the Painted Desert with a minimum of inconvenience and discomfort, we knew the beginning of the end had come. Luxurious limousines crowded with eager tourists stared at us curiously as they hurried along. One day there was a steady stream of automobiles and trucks in addition to the Harvey buses; a car stopped, and the occupants chatted with us in a friendly way. They told us that the caravan was hauling the cast and equipment which had just been used near Lees Ferry on the Colorado in the filming of Zane Grey's "Heritage of the Desert." The pleasantest person in the car was a large man with a bushy beard who pressed upon us some excellent sandwiches which they had had put up as their lunch. We did not learn until we reached their camp that night that our benefactor was Noah Beery.

Our last night on the desert we camped on the

summit of a high ridge overlooking the Painted
Desert from one side and what we termed Season
Valley from the other. Season Valley, because
just over the ridge are the glorious tints of
spring in the buttressing sand-banks on either
side; then, below, a deep stretch of green grass,
bear-grass, and hummocks of tufted grass which
typify summer; this picture is followed by the fall
tints of brown, yellow, and gold of the edge of
the Little Colorado; far beyond, winter—the
cold, snow-capped, black-walled horizon. Behind
us the Painted Desert. Afternoon: a half-horizon
view—the mesa's edge, some ten miles off, snow-
capped; below a series of spreading supports, a
violet cap breaks downward into five or six lines
of pink, which disintegrate in turn into twenty or
more spreading ribbons of brown; then the valley
floor of a sheen of orange, Chinese red, light
green, succeeded by a flow of silver sands, and
in the foreground our own ridge of black and
dark green. Sunset: the desert of a Spanish carpet merging yellows, reds, and greens; the last
rays show subdued tints below the horizon lights
of green, blue, gray, and black. Moonlight: now
the effect in the distance of a well spread pueblo

village bordering a murky river—silver moon-shafts upon adobe housetops. Sunrise: our desert a deep tan with no awakening touches of color, but Season Valley becomes a fluted bottom of red and white Bad Lands, succeeded by a mist-hidden river's edge, and the horizon silhouettes three huge turtles behind cloud folds.

It was hard to break that ever memorable camp and to leave the desert behind us. About noon we crossed the Little Colorado and were officially out of the Navajo Reservation, although the Navajo empire extends beyond the reservation boundaries. We had some difficulty in persuading our horses that the bridge was safe; it was un-doubtedly the first time that any of them had ever crossed such a structure. Immediately across the river is the Little Colorado Navajo Indian Trading Post, whitewashed and painted, ex-pensively furnished, a sign on the outside, "In-dian Rugs and Curios," and in general a totally un-Indian trading-post with prices correspond-ingly civilized. Truly we were again in White Man's Land. Here I sold my McClellan saddle, for which I had paid five dollars six months be-fore, to a Navajo for twice that sum. I mention

this fact with pride, for it is the only time that I
was ever able to worst an aborigine in a financial
transaction. I rode the last hundred miles bare-
back.

From the Little Colorado post we traveled to
the west until we reached Waterloo Hill. After
a terrific climb we were upon Tusayan plateau
and actually in the Grand Cañon region. That
day we passed the last *hogans* we were to see; we
were out of the Navajo empire. In the late afternoon of the same day we encountered a snow-
storm, and for the first time we were almost glad
that our trip was drawing to a close. We were
used to frost on our beds and did not mind finding the water in our canteens frozen solid, but
snow-storms were a little too much. Toward evening we arrived at a ranch-house which appeared
deserted. Casting discretion to the winds, we
made ourselves entirely at home. At 7 P.M. the
owner drove in. Like a true Westerner he accepted the situation gracefully and let us play
the hospitable hosts.

The next evening we were guests of Mr. Wil-
liam Randolph Hearst, or perhaps I should say
of the caretaker of his estate at Grand View

Point. It was there that we first saw the Great Sight. More has been written about the Grand Cañon of the Colorado than about any other one piece of scenery in America; countless authors and noted men have said that the cañon was indescribable and have then proceeded to prove it by writing a few thousand words about it. One cannot look into its colorful depths without a profound feeling of awe. It is said that a minister of the gospel on first gazing into its mystery fell on his knees and cried: "Holy! Holy! Holy! Lord God Almighty!" A cow-puncher arrived at the same time. He stared and then ejaculated: "Jesus Christ all hemlock!"

It was with strange and mingled feelings that we beheld El Tovar Hotel, the trains, and the Grand Cañon settlement in general. We had not seen so many white people for months; we had not seen a train for many months. Brave but bewildered, we wandered among the fashionably dressed people hurrying about in an effort to see the most sublime sight in America in twelve hours. They stared at us and drew back lest they approach too close. A few of them were brave enough to ask us questions about the wilds, and some had the effrontery to think that we were part of the scenery provided by Fred Harvey.

We decided that our first duty was to dispose of our horses. We found it a task indeed. Horses seemed to be a drug on the market; many told us that they would not take a horse as a gift at that time of the year. When a lady, gentleman, and child approached us and asked if Na-Deen was safe with children, we scented a prospective buyer, but it seemed that the child had been promised a ride, and that the El Tovar horses and mules were too large. Na-Deen was glad to oblige, and indeed it was a pleasure to serve such an attractive child. When Andy had guided her for a few minutes she said, "Father, perhaps it tires the gentleman to support me in this way." This rather overpowered us, coming from a little tot of three. It turned out that she was a child moving-picture actress, but not at all spoiled; we had never seen more charm or better manners. When they were leaving us, we said that if we were more permanently settled we would ask them to a camp supper. To our surprise they suggested that we get settled immediately, and they would provide the essentials for the supper.

And so we had guests to a supper of pancakes and macaroni. It developed that Mr. Hughes was also a Princetonian of an earlier vintage, and we held a real reunion. It sounded rather strange to hear "Going Back to Old Nassau" and "The Jungle Song" echoing in the pines of Tusayan Forest.

The following day we went to Rowe's Well Store to see what the prospects would be of selling our horses to the Havasupai Indians camped in that vicinity. We found them a dirty, ill tempered race. While traveling in this locality I had an adventure that Andy found amusing. It was a sort of Don Quixote argument with a supposedly automatic gate, and when Buck refused to halt at the crucial moment when I reached for the string, I was playfully dumped upon the sward. At last Andy sold Na-Deen to the white agent for the Havasupais, and we found a ranger who offered us fifty dollars for the other horses and our equipment.

Our equipment and horses being disposed of, we walked back to Grand Cañon. There we had considerable hair removed from our heads and faces before we dared apply for a room at the

Bright Angel Cottages. It seemed queer to live in a room, to have our meals prepared and served to us, and to sleep in a bed.

We spent two days wandering about the rim of the cañon. The view is different from each point, and each view differs according to the hour of the day. The distances are beyond comprehension. It hardly seems possible that it is thirteen miles across the cañon and that the fine thread you see at its bottom is the Colorado River, three hundred feet wide. We both wished that we had been able to visit the Grand Cañon a hundred years earlier, for we were unused to having our contemplation of the wonders of nature spoiled by crowds of chattering tourists; and then, too, one gets the feeling that the National Park Service has everything just a little too well regulated. You could hardly jump into the cañon if you wished to do so.

After we had walked down Bright Angel Trail to Tonto Plateau, we realized quite well that it is a long way down. We also decided that it is not always easy to go down a trail when the trail is as steep and twisting as Bright Angel. We crossed Tonto Plateau by way of Tonto Trail, and then again descended, this time to the river. The muddy Colorado whirling between the high walls of the Granite Gorge is a magnificent sight. The Kaibab Suspension Bridge provides a safe enough passage across the river, although it did feel extremely shaky. Just in time for supper, we arrived at the group of stone buildings in Bright Angel Cañon known as Phantom Ranch. The construction of these buildings was a noteworthy achievement. All the materials used, with the exception of the stone, and all the furnishings were carried down mule-back from the rim. It took more than seven thousand mule-loads to furnish the essentials for three buildings. The caretakers at Phantom Ranch lead a curious existence, shut off completely from the upper world. There is often as much as thirty degrees difference between the temperature at the ranch and the temperature at the rim; in the winter it is always warm and pleasant in Bright Angel Cañon, but in the summer the mercury rises to ninety-five degrees in the daytime, and at night the rocks radiate the heat they have collected during the day and the temperature often reaches one hundred and ten degrees.

The ascent to the outer world is toilsome in the extreme, and we were too worn out to bum our way to Williams as we had planned. And so we took the train, which was almost a novel sensation to both of us. Roy had not experienced this form of locomotion for ten months, and I for slightly longer.

We left the train at Williams to become knights of the road. We took the Old Trails Highway and started eastward. It was great fun; we came in contact with many types of persons. We did not walk very often, although many tourists appeared afraid to pick us up. At Adamana we stopped and took a twelve-mile hike to visit the Petrified Forests of Arizona. Prone upon the ground lie thousands of agatized pine and spruce tree-trunks. Some are two hundred feet long and five or six feet thick, but there are smaller pieces of all sizes and descriptions. The varieties of coloring transcend anything imaginable.

At last on a chill November day we arrived in Gallup, New Mexico. There we planned to separate—Roy to take the train for New York City, and I to return to the ranch at Ramah for a brief visit. But in Gallup we heard that a Navajo *Yei Bit Chai* was being held not a great distance to the north of Gallup, and we felt that it would be criminal to miss such an appropriate conclusion to our trip.

A day later we arrived at Thoreau, New Mexico, near which the *Yei Bit Chai* ceremonial was to be held. Our arrival was timely, for preparation had been completed, and the next day was to be the first of the ceremony.

XXIV

A SPOT more typical of the arid landscape of Arizona and New Mexico, or more suggestive of the primitive beauties and longings which haunt the land and its people, could not have been chosen for the celebration of this sacrament of the desert. The broad rolling valley, splotched with clumps of dwarf-cedar and carpeted with the fragrant sage, is limited on the one side by the heavily timbered slopes of the Zuñi Mountains and on the other by the glorious red and purple cliffs which terminate the vast table-land of Red Rock Mesa. In a valley within the valley is the medicine lodge, a conical structure of pine logs, and near-by is a square space set off by a palisade which is to serve as the communal cook-house. All about are the Navajos lithe and tall, clad in colors borrowed from the landscape of their desert home; they sit in family groups around the fire (for it is early on a late November morning and the sun has not yet taken the chill from the thin air) ; or, wrapped in blankets, they slowly go about preparations for the dance.

Near the medicine *hogan,* instructing the group of students who are to be his assistants, we find Hosteen Latsan Ih Begay, the officiating song-priest. I have yet to see a more striking figure; his features, of rather an Arabian cast, were regular and noble; his attire accentuated the picture of dignified but barbaric strength—the shirt of purple velvet, fastened with silver buttons, the twin medicine pouches, hanging from his shoulders, the scintillating belt composed of disks of hammered silver which confined his doeskin breeches; although more than past middle life, he still held himself to his full imposing stature, and one saw rippling under his velvet sleeves muscles that had torn the piñon from its roots.

He spoke, and his speech was not the lightly tripped, garrulous speech of Navajo youth; it was the slow, carefully weighed discourse of the elder statesman. He had heard of us, had heard little against us; but white men were prone to ridicule things sacred to the Indian, and for the Indian to expose his holies to the possibility of contempt was as displeasing as to ridicule them himself. He would consider, however. And by crier he summoned all who knew of us. We waited while Hosteen asked sharp incisive questions, and while incidents of our stay in Navajo land, but dimly remembered by us, were related.

At last our judge arose, and he delivered his decision in these words: "For many months you have lived among us, and now you are returning to your people. You are young; you will live many years; you will talk to many; you will tell them of us. Since ten generations has the white man talked to us of his religion. We know his beliefs; we do not want them. The white man knows not our religion, and yet he says that it is not good, that our ceremonies are unclean, that we must leave our gods and take his god. You white men do not pray, you grumble; but you shall see us here praying for nine days that our friend may regain health. I shall let you remain to see the most of what is to come, so that you will go back to your people to tell them that they must leave to us our gods."

During the day, we learned that Hasjelti Dail-jis, the dance of Hasjelti, is a "medicine sing," which is always held in the fall or winter of the year—"when the thunder sleeps." Its general purpose is to pray for the health of the "Dinne" (literally, "the people"—the name which these Indians give themselves; Navajo comes from the Spanish name for them—"Apaches del Navaju," "Apaches of the cultivated fields"). The specific purpose of this Yei Bit Chai was double: first, to heal the mastoid infection of an important member of the Tsia-a-Chini (people of the red rocks) clan, by name, Nas Jagi Yaye; second, to confer the seldom bestowed honor of adoption into the Navajo tribe upon Chissee Nez (the tall Apache), known to his white friends as Burton I. Staples. Mr. Staples has been a true friend of the Navajo; he is among the foremost of those who are earnestly endeavoring to assist in the perpetuation of their native arts and crafts in their primitive form, and he has rendered them distinguished services in their struggle with the government to keep their lands intact. It was significant to observe that the Navajo method for restoring a member of their own race to

health and for fitting a white man for membership in the tribe were identical. We were in-
debted to Mr. Staples for many kind words to
his Navajo brethren in our behalf.

After darkness that evening, the first ceremony began. The bright fire in the midst of the
medicine *hogan* showed the song-priest sitting
motionless facing the door. The sick man now
entered the *hogan* and was placed on a blanket
in front of the song-priest. Then entered the
deities Hasjelti and Hostjoghon, and we had an
unusual opportunity to see how aboriginal man
looks and acts in the awful presence of his gods,
for although those present realized that these
grotesque, half-naked, masked figures were only
men impersonating the gods, still so steeped were
they in the mysticism of the sacrament that, in
effect, Hasjelti and Hostjoghon, two of the awful Yei Bit Chai, were there in the *hogan*. The
face of Hasjelti was concealed by a mask of deer-
skin, which was surmounted by a head-dress of
turkey- and eagle-feathers; his principal gar-
ment was a deerskin mantle from which hung
medicine pouches of fox-skin; the rest of his body
was unclothed. Hostjoghon wore a mask of deer-

skin colored blue and a less elaborate head-dress; around his loins were kilts of red velvet with a silver belt. It was explained to us that the deer-skin used in the mantles and masks must be secured from deer which have been smothered to death; a deer is run down and secured with ropes; corn pollen is placed in the nostrils until the deer is smothered.

Hasjelti placed a wooden square over the head of the invalid, while Hostjoghon chanted a prayer, the significance of which we could not catch. Then entered Hostoboken, the water-spirit, and the goddess, Hostjoboard, both in clownish costume, bedecked with cedar spray. These personages entered and in alternation placed twelve gaming-rings on different parts of the sick man's body to expel the evil and to bring health. Then three rings were taken to each of the four points of the compass and buried at the foot of piñon-trees; this was done in order that the evil and the disease taken from the sick man's body might not remain to contaminate the *hogan.*

The weird hooting peculiar to Hasjelti, and the first day of the Yei Bit Chai was at an end.

On the second, third, fourth, and fifth days, ceremonies, complicated in their symbolism, yet externally similar to that of the first night, were performed day and night. Many songs and prayers, beautiful in imagery, were sung and chanted by the medicine-man, by his assistants, and by the personators of the gods.

At daylight of the sixth day preparations for a sand picture began. First, all the ashes from the fire which had been burning in the *hogan* were removed. Then common yellowish sand was carried in blankets to form a square about three inches deep and perhaps five feet in diameter.

Exactly at sunrise, work on the painting began. Four students did the actual work, while the medicine-man from his permanent seat at the west end of the lodge facing the east corrected them when some detail did not suit him. On the background of yellow sand, the colored sand was dropped from between the fingers in a seemingly careless manner and yet with marvelous accuracy. Each student used five colors of sand: gray-blue, black, red, yellow, and white. The painting was divided into four sections: the first pictured the destruction of all the people of the earth save one girl; the second pictured the girl bearing a daughter, whose father was the pitying water, and this daughter in turn was shown espoused by the rays of the rising sun, Naiyenesgani; the third division of the painting depicted the visit of their child to his father, the sun, and his exploits in slaying the monsters upon earth; the last section suggested how the earth was repeopled by the creation of men and women from ears of corn.

The work was finished about three o'clock in the afternoon. The song-priest then sprinkled sacred meal over the figures in the picture, and the curtain at the door was drawn back to admit the invalid, at whose entrance the medicine-man burst into a horrid chant to the accompaniment of a gourd rattle. The sick man first sprinkled the painting with meal, and then inhaled incense from the fire. At this point we were excluded from the *hogan*.

At the conclusion of the ritual, all those present who had aches or pains of any sort took sand from the painting and rubbed it upon the affected parts. The painting was then erased and the sand carried some distance from the *hogan* in blankets, for these are the two inviolable laws concerning the sand-painting: the sun must never set upon a completed painting, and no woman must ever look upon one. The setting sun was laid to rest with a weird chant, and the night was given over to feasting.

On the seventh and eighth days the order of business was the completion of two other sand-pictures and of attendant ceremonies. On the eighth day, when the painting was almost completed, men began to go through the various camps announcing that the children should be brought to a certain spot for the initiation ceremony. Shortly afterward, Hasjelti, dressed as usual, and Hostjoboard, her nude body painted white, left the medicine *hogan* for the scene of the initiation some two hundred yards east.

Perhaps sixty children were formally taken into full membership in the tribe at this time. They sat in a semicircle, with the mothers standing behind the girls and the fathers behind the boys, arranged according to age—the oldest boy being at the extreme left (facing the east) and so on down to the youngest boy; then came the oldest girl, with the girls extending in order of age to the extreme right of the circle. Both boys and girls covered their heads with their blankets.

When the children were finally in position, Hasjelti passed down the line, dropping sacred meal on them. Then he and Hostjoboard took position in front of the line, and one at a time the boys were brought forward. These children believed that the masked figures were deities, not simply impersonators. (Until after this initiation ceremony children are not permitted any knowledge of the inner mysteries of their religion.) Most of these boys shook—partly from the cold—but also, I am sure, from sheer terror. They stood head downward while Hasjelti formed a cross upon their breasts with the sacred meal. Then Hostjoboard struck them upon the breast with her Yucca swords. Hasjelti would then turn them toward the right until they faced the east, and made another cross upon their back, while Hostjoboard struck them twice upon the back with her swords. Again they were brought to face east. Hasjelti made crosses upon their arms and then their knees, and again Hostjoboard followed with blows with her swords, first with the sword in her right hand, then with the sword in her left. (It is said that the crosses symbolize the scalp knot.) As soon as a boy had gone through the chastisement, he returned to his seat and recovered, and the next boy in the line went forward. The boys initiated, the girls received the attention of the gods. The maidens were not forced to leave their seats; when Hasjelti and Hostjoboard approached them their heads were uncovered, and they sat motionless. Hasjelti marked a line of meal on each foot of the girl; Hostjoboard then placed two ears of yellow corn decorated with piñon sprays against the soles of their feet. In like manner five other parts of their bodies were first sprinkled with the meal, then touched with the corn. After all the girls had been thus treated Hasjelti and Hostjoboard again took place in front of the center of the line. The children were ordered to uncover and raise their heads. The deities then unmasked. It was indeed strange to see the varying expression on the faces of the children when they discovered the deception. Generally amazement, but on some faces one noticed just a little hint of indignation at having been thus imposed upon. Then Hostjoboard placed her mask upon the faces of all in the line. Great care was taken, for a slight misplacement would surely result in blindness. This done, she placed the mask of Hasjelti upon the faces of those in line. The man who had personated this god first sprinkled his mask and then Hostjoboard's with pollen. Hostjoboard then reversed the process. Then the first boy at the left end of the line came forth and sprinkled the masks. This was repeated until all in the line had done so. Great care was observed in this ceremony, for the slightest error on the part of the children would cause dire calamities.

An hour after the close of the initiation, an interesting ceremony took place in front of the medicine *hogan.* The theurgist and the sick man were seated a little to the right of the entrance. Two new deities together with Hasjelti had a part in this ceremony. They were Taadojaii and the goddess Yebahdi. Hasjelti was dressed as before. Taadojaii was nude save for a G-string; he was elaborately painted in red and white. In his right hand a gourd rattle, in his left a bow. The goddess wore ordinary squaw's dress. After many antics outside, the invalid entered the lodge, followed by the theurgist and the personators of the gods, who first removed their masks. Within, Na Ta Ji Ya Ye was placed upon the painting. In this case the picture was surrounded with twelve turkey-wands. I could obtain no exact account of what went on within, but the loud cries and hooting issuing from the lodge suggested something rather unusual.

On the ninth day the gathering assumed impressive proportions. For the previous twenty-four hours Navajos had been pouring in from all parts of the empire to join the not inconsiderable number which had already gathered, so that by noon of the ninth day there were two thousand present. To the Navajo the sacred ceremonies have a social as well as a religious significance; at these times clan councils and family gatherings are held. Camps were scattered over an extensive radius, and the communal cookhouse was quite overcrowded. An avenue of covered wagons lined the space directly in front of the medicine *hogans*. Everywhere a riot of color —the squaws in velvet waists and skirts of gay muslin outshone their men, who were forced to depend upon their blankets and jewelry for effect.

All day long the refrain of low-pitched chants could be heard issuing from the medicine *hogan,* where Latsan Ih Begay and his brethren held prayerful council. Outside, a great band of youths were preparing masks and costumes and gathering wood for the fires. In the afternoon all present gathered to be addressed by Chee Dodge, the richest and most influential of the Navajos. He led a discussion of the extension of the reservation and other matters pertaining to the general welfare. It was a good example of primitive democracy, very much like the New England town-meeting.

Shortly after dark the ceremonies began with a processional led by Latsan Ih Begay, who was indeed impressive as he moved with slow, majestic steps, chanting this prayer the while:[1]

> Medicine house!
> House made of purple dawn,
> House made of evening light,
> House made of dark cloud,

[1] Here I have consulted the translation of Dr. Matthews.

House made of male rain,
House made of dark mist,
House made of female rain,
House made of pollen!
Dark cloud is at the door.
The trail of it is dark cloud.
The crooked thunderbolt is high upon it.

Male deity!
Your offering I make.
I have prepared a smoke for you.
Restore our hearts for us.
Restore our legs for us.
Restore our minds for us.
Restore our bodies for us.
Restore the sounds for us.

Happily may I walk.
Happily, with abundant dark clouds, may I walk.
Happily, with abundant showers, may I walk.
Happily may I walk.

Being as it used to be long ago, may I walk.
May it be beautiful before me.
May it be beautiful behind me.
May it be beautiful above me.
May it be beautiful all around me.
In beauty it is finished.
In beauty it is finished.

He was followed by Hasjelti and four Etsethle
(the first ones), who represented corn, rain,

vegetation, and corn-pollen. Their blue masks were topped with a feather head-dress, and they wore loin-skirts from which hung fox-skins; their bodies were painted white, and in their right hands they carried gourd rattles. Twenty feet from the *hogan*, the procession halted, while the song-priest turned to the four Etsethle and chanted a short prayer. Then there was a long monotonous chant by the Etsethle, which reminded the people that corn is their food; that for rain Hasjelti must be prayed to; that, if vegetation is to grow, the sun must warm the earth. The song-priest and the invalid then joined in a prayer to the Etsethle. The invalid seated himself in front of the lodge, but the song-priest remained standing, while the Etsethle indulged in an esoteric dance to the accompaniment of ear-rending hooting by Hasjelti.

A short while afterward came another procession led by the assistant song-priest, followed by twelve dancers who represented the original man and woman of the world six times reduplicated. The singing in a falsetto key and the quick movements of the dancers were beyond description. The effect was fascinating, yet patently barbaric.

All night long the dance continued. To the superficial observer there was little variation in the dance, save in the number of those taking part, and in the occasional appearance of a woman; but each chant and each new figure quite evidently had a real meaning to the native spectators.

Just as the sun was rising, the dance terminated in the exquisite Bluebird Song. All the dancers gathered in a circle and, after removing their masks, reverently sang this beautiful lyric, which relates the legend of the creation. It is totally different from the vast body of Amerindian songs, being melodious and sung softly in a very low key. When the singing was done, the masks had but to be sprinkled with pollen, and the ceremony of Hasjelti Dailjis was at an end. Three hours later it all seemed as if by magic, and there was nothing left to conjure with save the ashes of the fires.

Sorrowfully a day later I watched Andy board the limited for Chicago, to return, as he expressed it, to "the real, the practical, the sane, to respectable citizens, to the Woman's Christian Temperance Union and Civic Betterment Clubs." And this then was the end of our glorious adventure. But, oh, long, long, will we hear the hoots of the Yei Bit Chai; always we can see Nonne-zoche Not-se-lid gracefully spanning the cañon; the memories of our camp-fires, of our horses, of our friends, white and red, are as vivid as they were yesterday and will be to-morrow. Au revoir, Land of Enchantment! You were very kind to us.